2nd International Workshop on Natural Language Generation and the Semantic Web (WebNLG 2016)

Edinburgh, Scotland
6 September 2016

ISBN: 978-1-5108-3115-5

WebNLG 2016

Proceedings of the
2nd International Workshop
on
Natural Language Generation
and the Semantic Web

6 September 2016
Edinburgh, Scotland

WebNLG 2016 is sponsored by:

the French National Research Agency Project ANR-14-CE24-0033 "Generating Text from Semantic Web Data" (WebNLG)

Introduction

It is with great pleasure that we present the current volume of papers accepted for presentation at the 2nd International Workshop on Natural Language Generation and the Semantic Web to be held in Edinburgh, Scotland on September 6th, 2016.

The WebNLG 2016 workshop is a follow up to a first WebNLG workshop which was held in Nancy on June 12th, 2015. Funded by the French ANR WebNLG Project, these two workshops aim to provide a forum for presenting and discussing research on Natural Language Generation from Semantic Web data.

WebNLG 2016 invited submissions on all topics related to Natural Language Generation and the Semantic Web. We received 14 submissions from all over the world. Of these 5 long papers and 8 short papers were accepted for presentation. The long papers will be presented orally, and the short papers as posters.

In addition, WebNLG 2016 hosts an Invited talk by Roberto Navigli from Sapienza University (Rome, Italy) on the past, present and future of Babelnet .

We are indebted to the authors and to the members of our program committee for their work which contributed to make for a very enjoyable workshop. We are also delighted that Roberto Navigli agreed to give an invited talk at WebNLG 2016. Last but not least, many thanks go to the local organisation team, Emilie Colin, Bikash Gyawali, Mariem Mahfoudh and Laura Perez-Beltrachini for handling the website and the preparation of the meeting.

Claire Gardent and Aldo Gangemi
Program co-Chairs for WebNLG 2016

Program Chairs:

Aldo Gangemi, Université Paris 13, Paris (France)
Claire Gardent, CNRS/LORIA, Nancy (France)

Organisation Committee:

Bikash Gyawali CNRS/LORIA, Nancy (France). Chair.
Laura Perez-Beltrachini CNRS/LORIA, Nancy (France), Chair.
Émilie Colin, CNRS/LORIA , Nancy (France), Webmaster.
Mariem Mahfoudh, CNRS/LORIA, Nancy (France)

Program Committee:

Mehwish Alam, LIPN Université Paris 13 (France)
Nathalie Aussenac-Gilles, CNRS/IRIT Toulouse (France)
Valerio Basile, INRIA, Sophia Antipolis (France)
Gerard Casamayor, Universitat Pompeu Fabra (Spain)
Vinay Chaudhri, SRI International, Menlo Park (USA)
Mathieu Dacquin, The Open University (UK)
Claudia d'Amato, Bari University (Italy)
Brian Davis, INSIGHT, Galway (Ireland)
Marc Dymetman, XRCE, Grenoble (France)
Enrico Franconi, KRDB, Bolzano (Italy)
Bikash Gyawali, CNRS/LORIA, Nancy (France)
Guy Lapalme, RALI / Université de Montréal (Canada)
Shao-Fen Liang, Kings College London (UK)
Elena Lloret, University of Alicante (Spain)
Vanessa Lopez, IBM Ireland Research Lab, Dublin (Ireland)
Mariem Mahfoudh, CNRS/LORIA, Nancy (France)
Yassine M'rabet, U.S. National Library of Medicine, Bethesda (USA)
Shashi Narayan, University of Edinburgh (UK)
Axel-Cyrille Ngonga-Ngomo, University of Leipzig (Germany)
Laura Perez-Beltrachini, CNRS/LORIA, Nancy (France)
Sergio Tessaris, KRDB, Bolzano (Italy)
Allan Third, The Open University (UK)
Yannick Toussaint, INRIA/LORIA, Nancy (France)
Christina Unger, CITEC, Universitt Bielefeld (Germany)

Invited Speaker

Roberto Navigli, Sapienza Università di Roma, Roma, Italy

BabelNet: past, present and future

In this talk I will overview work done in my group at the Linguistic Computing Laboratory in the Computer Science Department of the Sapienza University of Rome which addresses key problems in multilingual lexical semantics. I will start from a brief introduction to BabelNet, the largest multilingual semantic network and encyclopedic dictionary covering 14 million concepts and entities, and 271 languages, also at the core of the so-called Linguistic Linked Open Data cloud. I will move on to Word Sense Disambiguation and Entity Linking in arbitrary languages with "zero training" (Babelfy) and then present recent latent and explicit vector representations of meaning which obtain state-of-the-art results in several NLP tasks. Finally, I will present my plan for making BabelNet a sustainable, continuously-improved resource. This is joint work with several people from my NLP group at Sapienza.

Roberto Navigli is an Associate Professor in the Department of Computer Science of the Sapienza University of Rome. He was awarded the Marco Somalvico 2013 AI*IA Prize for the best young researcher in AI. He was the first Italian recipient of an ERC Starting Grant in computer science (2011-2016), and a co-PI of a Google Focused Research Award on Natural Language Understanding. In 2015 he received the META prize for groundbreaking work in overcoming language barriers with BabelNet. His research lies in the field of multilingual Natural Language Processing. Currently he is an Associate Editor of the Artificial Intelligence Journal.

Table of Contents

Conference Program

Tuesday, September 6, 2016

9:00–10:00   Invited Talk

BabelNet: Past, Present and Future
Roberto Navigli

10:00–10:45   **Posters**
Analysing the Integration of Semantic Web Features for Document Planning across Genres
Marta Vicente and Elena Lloret

Building a System for Stock News Generation in Russian
Liubov Nesterenko

Comparing the Template-Based Approach to GF: the case of Afrikaans
Lauren Sanby, Ion Todd and C. Maria Keet

Content Selection as Semantic-Based Ontology Exploration
Laura Perez-Beltrachini, Claire Gardent, Anselme Revuz and Saptarashmi Bandy-opadhyay

Content Selection through Paraphrase Detection: Capturing different Semantic Realisations of the Same Idea
Elena Lloret and Claire Gardent

Generating Sets of Related Sentences from Input Seed Features
Cristina Barros and Elena Lloret

Processing Document Collections to Automatically Extract Linked Data: Semantic Storytelling Technologies for Smart Curation Workflows
Peter Bourgonje, Julian Moreno Schneider, Georg Rehm and Felix Sasaki

ReadME Generation from an OWL Ontology Describing NLP Tools
Driss Sadoun, Satenik Mkhitaryan, Damien Nouvel and Mathieu Valette

Oral presentations

10:45–11:05   *Generating Paraphrases from DBPedia using Deep Learning*
Amin Sleimi and Claire Gardent

11:05–11:25   *Aligning Texts and Knowledge Bases with Semantic Sentence Simplification*
Yassine Mrabet, Pavlos Vougiouklis, Halil Kilicoglu, Claire Gardent, Dina Demner-Fushman, Jonathon Hare and Elena Simperl

Generating Sets of Related Sentences From Input Seed Features

Cristina Barros
Department of Software
and Computing Systems
University of Alicante
Apdo. de Correos 99
E-03080, Alicante, Spain
cbarros@dlsi.ua.es

Elena Lloret
Department of Software
and Computing Systems
University of Alicante
Apdo. de Correos 99
E-03080, Alicante, Spain
elloret@dlsi.ua.es

1 Introduction

The Semantic Web (SW) can provide Natural Language Generation (NLG) with technologies capable to facilitate access to structured Web data. This type of data can be useful to this research area, which aims to automatically produce human utterances, in its different subtasks, such as in the content selection or its structure.

NLG has been widely applied to several fields, for instance to the generation of recommendations (Lim-Cheng et al., 2014). However, generation systems are currently designed for very specific domains (Ramos-Soto et al., 2015) and predefined purposes (Ge et al., 2015). The use of SW's technologies can facilitate the development of more flexible and domain independent systems, that could be adapted to the target audience or purposes, which would considerably advance the state of the art in NLG. The main objective of this paper is to propose a multidomain and multilingual statistical approach focused on the surface realisation stage using factored language models. Our proposed approach will be tested in the context of two different domains (fairy tales and movie reviews) and for the English and Spanish languages, in order to show its appropriateness to different non-related scenarios. The main novelty studied in this approach is the generation of related sentences (sentences with related topics) for different domains, with the aim to achieve cohesion between sentences and move forward towards the generation of coherent and cohesive texts. The approach can be flexible enough thanks to the use of an input seed feature that guides all the generation process. Within our scope, the seed feature can be seen as an abstract object that will determine how the sentence will be in terms of content. For example, this seed feature could be a phoneme, a property or a RDF triple from where the proposed approach

could generate a sentence.

2 Factored Language Models and NLG

Factored language models (FLM) are an extension of language models proposed in (Bilmes and Kirchhoff, 2003). In this model, a word is viewed as a vector of k factors such that $w_t \equiv \{f_t^1, f_t^2, \ldots, f_t^K\}$. These factors can be anything, including the Part-Of-Speech (POS) tag, lemma, stem or any other lexical, syntactic or semantic feature. Once a set of factors is selected, the main objective of a FLM is to create a statistical model $P(f|f_1, \ldots, f_N)$ where the prediction of a feature f is based on N parents $\{f_1, \ldots, f_N\}$. For example, if w represents a word token and t represents a POS tag, the expression $P(w_i|w_{i-2}, w_{i-1}, t_{i-1})$ provides a model to determine the current word token, based on a traditional n-gram model together with the POS tag of the previous word. Therefore, in the development of such models there are two main issues to consider: 1) choose an appropriate set of factors, and 2) find the best statistical model over these factors.

In recent years, FLM have been used in several areas of Computational Linguistics, mostly in machine translation (Crego, 2010; Axelrod, 2006) and speech recognition (Tachbelie et al., 2011; Vergyri et al., 2004). To a lesser extent, they have been also employed for generating language, mainly in English. This is the case of the BAGEL system (Mairesse and Young, 2014), where FLM (with semantic concepts as factors) are used to predict the semantic structure of the sentence that is going to be generated; or OpenCCG (White and Rajkumar, 2009), a surface realisation tool, where FLM (with POS tag and supertags as factors) are used to score partial and complete realisations to be later selected. More recently, FLM (with POS tag, word and lemma as factors) were used to

Proceedings of the 2nd International Workshop on Natural Language Generation and the Semantic Web (WebNLG), pages 1–4,
Edinburgh, Scotland, September 6th, 2016. ©2016 Association for Computational Linguistics

rank generated sentences in Portuguese (Novais and Paraboni, 2012).

The fact of generating connected and related sentences is a challenge in itself, and, to the best of our knowledge there is not any research with the restriction of containing words with a specific seed feature, thus leading to a more flexible NLG approach that could be easily adapted to different purposes, domains and languages.

3 Generating Related Sentences Using FLM

We propose an almost-fully language independent statistical approach focused on the surface realisation stage and based on over-generation and ranking techniques, which can generate related sentences for different domains. This is achieved through the use of input seed features, which are abstract objects (e.g., a phoneme, a semantic class, a domain, a topic, or a RDF triple) that will guide the generation process in relation to the most suitable vocabulary for a given purpose or domain.

Starting from a training corpus, a test corpus and a seed feature as the input of our approach, a FLM will be learnt over the training corpus and a bag of words with words related with the seed feature will be obtained from the test corpus. Then, based on the FLM and bag of words previously obtained, the process will generate several sentences for a given seed feature, which will be subsequently ranked. This process will prioritise the selection of words from the bag of words to guarantee that the generated sentences will contain the maximum number of words related with the input seed feature. Once several sentences are generated, only one of them will be selected based on the sentence probability, that will be computed using a linear combination of FLMs.

When a sentence is generated, we will perform post-tagging, syntactic parsing and/or semantic parsing to identify several linguistic components of the sentence (such as the subject, named entities, etc.) that will also provide clues about its structural shape. This will allow us to generate the next sentence taking into account the shape of the previous generated one, and the structure we want to obtain (e.g., generating sentences about the same subject with complementary information).

4 Experimental scenarios and resources

For our experimentation, we want to consider two different scenarios, NLG for assistive technologies and sentiment-based NLG. Within the first scenario, the experimentation will be focused on the domain of fairy tales. The purpose in this scenario is the generation of stories that can be useful for therapies in dyslalia speech therapies (Rvachew et al., 1999). Dyslalia is a disorder in phoneme articulation, so the repetition of words with problematic phonemes can improve their pronunciation. Therefore, in this scenario, the selected seed feature will be a phoneme, where the generated sentences will contain a large number of words with a concrete phoneme. As corpora, a collection of Hans Christian Andersen tales will be used due to the fact that its vocabulary is suitable for young audience, since dyslalia affects more to the child population, having a 5-10% incidence among them (Conde-Guzón et al., 2014).

Regarding the second scenario, the experimentation will be focused on generating opinionated sentences (i.e., sentences with a positive or negative polarity) in the domain of movie reviews. Taking into account that there are many Websites where users express their opinions by means of non-linguistic rates in the form of numeric values or symbols[1], the generation of this kind of sentences can be used to generate sentences from visual numeric rates. Given this proposed scenario, we will employ the Spanish Movie Reviews corpus[2] and the Sentiment Polarity Dataset (Pang and Lee, 2004) as our corpora for Spanish and English, respectively.

In order to learn the FLM that will be used during the generation, we will use SRILM (Stolcke, 2002), a software which allows to build and apply statistical language models, which also includes an implementation of FLM.

In addition, Freeling language analyser (Padró and Stanilovsky, 2012) will be also employed to tag the corpus with lexical information as well as to perform the syntactic analysis and the name entity recognition of the generated sentences. Furthermore, in order to obtain and evaluate the polarity for our second proposed domain, we will employ the sentiment analysis classifier described and developed in (Fernández et al., 2013).

---

[1] An example of such a Website can be found at: http://www.reviewsdepeliculas.com/

[2] http://www.lsi.us.es/ fermin/corpusCine.zip

5 Preliminary Experimentation

As an initial experimentation, we design a simple grammar (based on the basic clause structure that divides a sentence into subject and predicate) to generate sets of sentences which will have related topics (nouns) with each other, since these topics will appear within the set.

In this case, we generate the sentences with the structure shown in Figure 1, where we use the direct object of the previous generated sentences as the subject for the following sentence to be produced, so that we can obtain a preliminary set of related sentences.

The words contained in these preliminary related sentences are in a lemma form since this configuration proved to works better than others, being able to be further inflected in order to obtain several inflections of the sentences from where the final generated one will be chosen.

$$S \rightarrow NP\ VP$$
$$NP \rightarrow D\ N$$
$$VP \rightarrow V\ NP$$

Figure 1: Basic clause structure grammar.

With this structure we generated a set of 3 related sentences for each phoneme in both languages, Spanish and English, and another set of 3 related sentences for positive and negative polarities in the languages mentioned before.

These sentences have the structure seen above and were ranked according to the approach outlined in section 3 being the linear combination of FLM as follows: $P(w_i) = \lambda_1 P(f_i|f_{i-2}, f_{i-1}) + \lambda_2 P(f_i|p_{i-2}, p_{i-1}) + \lambda_3 P(p_i|f_{i-2}, f_{i-1})$, where f can be can be either a lemma and a word, p refers to a POS tag, and λ_i are set $\lambda_1 = 0.25$, $\lambda_2 = 0.25$ and $\lambda_3 = 0.5$. These values were empirically determined.

Some examples of the generated sentences for the first scenario, concerning the generation of sentences for assistive technologies, is shown in Figure 2. In some of the sets of generated sentences, the same noun appears as a direct object in both, the first and the third generated sentences for that set. On the other hand, examples of sets of sentences generated in both, English and Spanish, for the second experimentation scenario (movie reviews domain) are shown in the Figure 3.

Generally, the generated sentences for our two experimentation scenarios, conform to the specified in section 4, although in some cases the verbs

Spanish
Phoneme: /n/
Cuánto cosa tener nuestro pensamiento.
(How much thing have our thinking.)
Cuánto pensamiento tener nuestro corazón.
(How much thought have our heart.)
Cuánto corazón tener nuestro pensamiento.
(How much heart have our thinking.)

English
Phoneme: /s/
These child say the princess.
Each princess say the shadow.
Each shadow pass this story.

Figure 2: Example generated sentences for the assistive technologies scenario.

in these sentences need the inclusion of preposition in order to bring more correctness to the generated sentences.

Spanish
Polarity: Negative
Este defecto ser el asesino.
(This defect being the murderer.)
Su asesino ser el policía.
(His murderer be the police.)
El policía interpretar este papel.
(The police play this role.)

English
Polarity: Negative
Many critic reject the plot.
This plot confuse the problem.
The problem lie this mess.

Figure 3: Example generated sentences for movie reviews domain in our second scenario.

At this stage, these preliminary set of generated related sentences are a promising step towards our final goal, since the number of words with the seed feature among the sentences are more than the number of words of the sentences, meeting the overall objective for which they were generated. Although the grammar used in the generation of these sentences only captures the basic structure for the two languages studied, the use of more complex grammars could give us insights to improve some aspects of the generation of these preliminary sentences in the future.

6 Ongoing research steps

In order to enrich this approach and meet the final goal, we want to deeply research into some of the representation languages used by the SW, such as OWL, as well as its technologies, that fit our proposed approach. Obtaining information related to a certain topic is tough without using any kind of external technology, so the employing of SW languages, such as RDF, can facilitate us accessing this type of information.

In the future, we would like to analyse how the generated sentences could be connected using discourse markers. We also would like to test the generation of sentences using other structural shapes, such as sharing the same subject or sentences sharing the same predicative objects with different subjects. The generation of related sentences is not a trivial task, being the cohesion and coherence between sentences very hard to be checked automatically. So, in that case, we plan to conduct an exhaustive user evaluation of the generated sentences using crowdsourcing platforms.

Acknowledgments

This research work has been funded by the University of Alicante, Generalitat Valenciana, Spanish Government and the European Commission through the projects GRE13-15, PROM-ETEOII/2014/001, TIN2015-65100-R, TIN2015-65136-C2-2-R, and FP7-611312, respectively.

References

Amittai Axelrod. 2006. Factored language models for statistical machine translation. master thesis. university of edinburgh.

Jeff A. Bilmes and Katrin Kirchhoff. 2003. Factored language models and generalized parallel backoff. In *Proceedings of the 2003 Conference of the North American Chapter of the Association for Computational Linguistics on Human Language Technology: Companion Volume of the Proceedings of HLT-NAACL 2003–short Papers - Volume 2*, pages 4–6.

Pablo Conde-Guzón, Pilar Quirós-Expósito, María Jesús Conde-Guzón, and María Teresa Bartolomé-Albistegui. 2014. Perfil neuropsicológico de niños con dislalias: alteraciones mnésicas y atencionales. *Anales de Psicología*, 30:1105 – 1114.

François Crego, Josep M.and Yvon. 2010. Factored bilingual n-gram language models for statistical machine translation. *Machine Translation*, 24(2):159–175.

Javi Fernández, Yoan Gutiérrez, José Manuel Gómez, Patricio Martínez-Barco, Andrés Montoyo, and Rafael Muñoz. 2013. Sentiment analysis of spanish tweets using a ranking algorithm and skipgrams. *Proc. of the TASS workshop at SEPLN 2013*, pages 133–142.

Tao Ge, Wenzhe Pei, Heng Ji, Sujian Li, Baobao Chang, and Zhifang Sui. 2015. Bring you to the past: Automatic generation of topically relevant event chronicles. In *Proceedings of the 53rd Annual Meeting of the Association for Computational Linguistics and the 7th International Joint Conference on Natural Language Processing*, pages 575–585, July.

Natalie R. Lim-Cheng, Gabriel Isidro G. Fabia, Marco Emil G. Quebral, and Miguelito T. Yu. 2014. Shed: An online diet counselling system. In *DLSU Research Congress 2014*.

François Mairesse and Steve Young. 2014. Stochastic language generation in dialogue using factored language models. *Comput. Linguist.*, 40(4):763–799.

Eder Miranda Novais and Ivandré Paraboni. 2012. Portuguese text generation using factored language models. *Journal of the Brazilian Computer Society*, 19(2):135–146.

Lluís Padró and Evgeny Stanilovsky. 2012. Freeling 3.0: Towards wider multilinguality. In *Proceedings of the Eight International Conference on Language Resources and Evaluation*.

Bo Pang and Lillian Lee. 2004. A sentimental education: Sentiment analysis using subjectivity summarization based on minimum cuts. In *Proceedings of the ACL*.

A. Ramos-Soto, A. J. Bugarn, S. Barro, and J. Taboada. 2015. Linguistic descriptions for automatic generation of textual short-term weather forecasts on real prediction data. *IEEE Transactions on Fuzzy Systems*, 23(1):44–57.

Susan Rvachew, Susan Rafaat, and Monique Martin. 1999. Stimulability, speech perception skills, and the treatment of phonological disorders. *American Journal of Speech-Language Pathology*, 8(1):33–43.

Andreas Stolcke. 2002. Srilm - an extensible language modeling toolkit. In *Proceedings International Conference on Spoken Language Processing, vol 2.*, pages 901–904.

Martha Yifiru Tachbelie, Solomon Teferra Abate, and Wolfgang Menzel, 2011. *Human Language Technology. Challenges for Computer Science and Linguistics: 4th Language and Technology Conference*, chapter Morpheme-Based and Factored Language Modeling for Amharic Speech Recognition, pages 82–93. Springer Berlin Heidelberg.

Dimitra Vergyri, Katrin Kirchhoff, Kevin Duh, and Andreas Stolcke. 2004. Morphology-based language modeling for arabic speech recognition. In *INTERSPEECH*, volume 4, pages 2245–2248.

Michael White and Rajakrishnan Rajkumar. 2009. Perceptron reranking for ccg realization. In *Proceedings of the 2009 Conference on Empirical Methods in Natural Language Processing*, pages 410–419. Association for Computational Linguistics.

A Repository of Frame Instance Lexicalizations for Generation

Valerio Basile

Université Côte d'Azur, Inria, CNRS, I3S, France

`valerio.basile@inria.fr`

Abstract

Robust, statistical Natural Language Generation from Web knowledge bases is hindered by the lack of text-aligned resources. We aim to fill this gap by presenting a method for extracting knowledge from natural language text, and encode it in a format based on frame semantics and ready to be distributed in the Linked Open Data space. We run an implementation of such methodology on a collection of short documents and build a repository of frame instances equipped with fine-grained lexicalizations. Finally, we conduct a pilot stody to investigate the feasibility of an approach to NLG based on said resource. We perform error analysis to assess the quality of the resource and manually evaluate the output of the NLG prototype.

1 Introduction

Statistical Natural Language Generation, generally speaking, is based on learning a mapping between natural language expressions (words, phrases, sentences) and abstract representations of their meaning or syntactic structure. In fact, such representations vary greatly in their degree of abstraction, from shallow syntactic trees to full-fledged logical formulas, depending on factors like downstream applications and the role of the generation module in a larger framework.

In order to be useful for statistical generation, the abstract representation needs to be aligned with the surface form. Depending on the format, the level of abstraction and the target degree of granularity of the alignment, it may be more or less straightforward to produce a collection of pairs <abstract representation, surface form>. Moreover, statistical methods typically need a large number of examples to properly learn a mapping and generalize efficiently.

While several resources have been successfully employed as training material for statistical NLG (see the related work section), they lack a direct link with world knowledge. Linked Open Data resources, in particular general knowledge bases such as DBpedia[1], on the other hand, are not straightfoward to use as a basis for generation, while at the same time they are rich in extra-linguistic information such as type hierarchy and semantic relations. Having the entities and concepts of an abstract meaning representation linked to a knowledge base allows a generator to use all the information coming from links to other resources in the LOD cloud. Such kind of input to a NLG pipeline is therefore richer than word-based structures, although its increased level of abstraction makes the generation process more complex.

Shifting the level of abstraction, the representation format must be changed accordingly. In the case of many formats proposed in the literature (e.g., the format of the Surface Realization shared task), the input for NLG is made of structures closely resembling sentences. The notion of sentence, however, might not be adequate anymore when the abstract representation of meaning aims to be fit for the standards of the Web. A good compromise is a representation based on frame semantics (Fillmore, 1982). A *frame* is a unit of meaning denoting a situation of a particular type, e.g., *Operate_vehicle*. Attached to the frame there are a number of *frame elements*, indicating roles that the entities involved in the frame can play, e.g., *Driver* or *Vehicle*. Rouces et al. (2015) proposes a LOD version of frame semantics implemented in the resource called FrameBase, essentially a scheme for representing instances of frames and frame ele-

---

[1] `http://dbpedia.org`

Proceedings of the 2nd International Workshop on Natural Language Generation and the Semantic Web (WebNLG), pages 5–12,
Edinburgh, Scotland, September 6th, 2016. ©2016 Association for Computational Linguistics

ments in a Web-based format. The FrameBase project also produced a repository of instances created by automatically translating existing Web resources. Moreover, they made available a large set of *(de)reification rules*, that is, bidirectional rules to convert between binary relations and frame-based representations. For instance, the binary relation *drivesVehicle* can be transformed by a reification rule into a *Operate_vehicle* frame with the two members of the original relation filling in the roles of *Driver* and *Vehicle*. The reification mechanism provides an interesting use case for NLG: if a system is able to generate natural langauge from a frame instance, then it is also able to generate from the corresponding binary relation.

In this paper, we present an ongoing work towards the construction of a domain-agnostic, LOD-compliant knowledge base of semantic frame instances. Frames, roles and entities are aligned to natural language words and phrases that express them, extracted from a large corpus of text. Thanks to this alignment, the resource can be used to create lexicalizations for new, unseen configurations of entities and frames.

2   Related Work

Several resources exists have been used to train a statistical generator to learn lexicalizations for various types of representations The Surface Realization Shared Task (Belz et al., 2011), for instance, provides a double dataset of shallow and deep input representations obtained by preprocessing the CoNNL 2008 Shared Task data (Surdeanu et al., 2008). Resources used for NLG include including the Penn Treebank (Marcus et al., 1993) for Probabilistic Lexical Functional Grammar (Cahill and Genabith, 2006) and CCGBank (Hockenmaier and Steedman, 2007) for Combinatory Categorial Grammar syntax trees (White et al., 2007). More recently, the Groningen Meaning Bank (Basile et al., 2012) has been proposed as a resource for NLG from abstract meaning representations, leveraging the fine-grained alignment between logical forms and their respective surface forms given by the Discourse Representation Graph formalism (Basile and Bos, 2013).

The process of generating natural language from databases of structured information, including ones following Web standards, has been studied in the past, although often in specific application-oriented contexts. Bouayad-Agha et al. (2012) propose an architecture as a basis for generation made of three RDF/OWL ontologies, separation the domain knowledge from the communication knowledge. Gyawali and Gardent (2014) propose a statistical approach to NLG fro mknowledge bases based on tree adjoining grammars. WordNet is relatively less used for generation purposes. Examples of the use of Wordnet in the context of NLG include the methods to address specific NLG-related tasks proposed by Jing (1998) and the algorithm for lexical choice of Basile (2014).

3   Aligning Text and Semantics

Basile and Bos (2013) devise a strategy to align arbitrary natural languages expressions to formal representation of their meaning, encoded as Discourse Representation Structures (DRS, Kamp and Reyle (1993)). DRSs are logical formulas comprising predicates and relations over discourse referents. For the English language, we are able to obtain DRSs for a given text using the C&C tools collection of linguistic analysis tools (Curran et al., 2007), which includes Boxer (Bos, 2008), a rule-based system that builds DRSs on top of the CCG parse tree produced by the C&C parser. Boxer implements *Neo-davidsonian* representations of meaning, that is, formulas centered around *events* to which participant entities are connected by filling *thematic roles*. Figure 1 shows an example of DRS for the sentence "A robot is driving the car" as produced by Boxer. In this example the Neo-davidsonian semantics is evident: the ROBOT is the AGENT of the event DRIVE, while the CAR is the THEME.

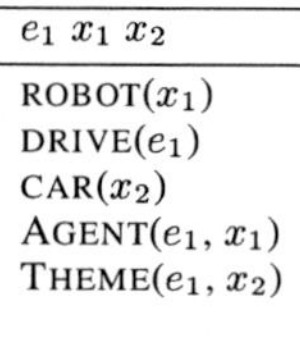

Figure 1: DRS representing the meaning of the sentence "A robot is driving the car"

The alignment method proposed by Basile and Bos (2013) is based on a translation of format from DRS into a Discourse Representation Graph (DRG), where the semantic information is preserved but expressed in a flat, non recursive formalism. The surface form is then aligned at the word level to the appropriate tuples. Figure 2 shows the DRG corresponding to the DRS in Figure 1, where the alignment with the surface form is contained in the two rightmost columns. For the details of how the alignment is encoded we refer the reader to the aforementioned paper (Basile and Bos, 2013).

k_1	referent	x_1	1	[A]
k_1	referent	e_1		
k_1	referent	x_2	1	[the]
k_1	event	DRIVE		
k_1	concept	ROBOT		
k_1	role	AGENT		
k_1	concept	CUSTOMER		
k_1	role	THEME		
ROBOT	instance	x_1	2	[robot]
DRIVE	instance	e_1	2	[is, driving]
AGENT	internal	e_1	1	
AGENT	external	x_1		
CAR	instance	x_2	2	[car]
THEME	internal	e_1	3	
THEME	external	x_2		

Figure 2: DRG aligned with the surface form, representing the meaning of the sentence "A robot is driving the car".

In order for the semantic representations, and their alignment to the surface, to be useful in contexts such as knowledge representation and automatic reasoning, these logical forms need to be linked to some kind of knowledge base. Otherwise, the predicate symbols in a DRG like the one depicted in Figure 2 are just interchangeable symbols (although Boxer uses lemmas for predicate names) devoid of meaning.

Popular resources in the LOD ecosystem are well-suited for serving as knowledge bases for grounding the symbols: WordNet (Miller, 1995) can be used to represent concepts and events, while DBPedia has a very large coverage for named entities. FrameNet (Baker et al., 1998), an inventory of frames and frame elements inspired by Fillmore's frame semantics (Fillmore, 1982), has a structure that superimposes easily to the neo-Davidsonian semantics of Boxer's DRGs. The inventory of thematic roles used by Boxer is taken from VerbNet (Schuler, 2005). By linking the discourse referents representing concepts in a DRG to WordNet synsets, entities to DBpedia and events to FrameNet frames we are able to extract complete representations of frames from natural language text linked to LOD knowledge bases.

4   Collecting Frame Lexicalizations

We developed a pipeline of NLP tools to automatically extract instances of frames from the text. The pipeline comprises the C&C tools and Boxer, a module for word sense disambiguation and a module for entity linking. The two latter modules can be configured to use different external software to perform their task.

The analysis of a text consists in the following steps:

1. Run the C&C tools and Boxer, saving both its XML and DRG output. The XML output of Boxer contains, for each predicates of the DRS that has been constructed, a link to the part of the surface form that introduced it.

2. Run the WSD and entity linking components, preserving the same tokenization. The software then uses the links to the text provided by Boxer to map the word senses and DBpedia entities to the DRS predicates.

3. The word senses corresponding to events are mapped to FrameNet frames, using the mapping provided by Rouces et al. (2015). The VerbNet roles are converted into FrameNet roles using the mapping provided by Loper et al. (2007).

4. The partial surface forms in the DRG output of Boxer are attached to the frames, semantic roles and frame elements.

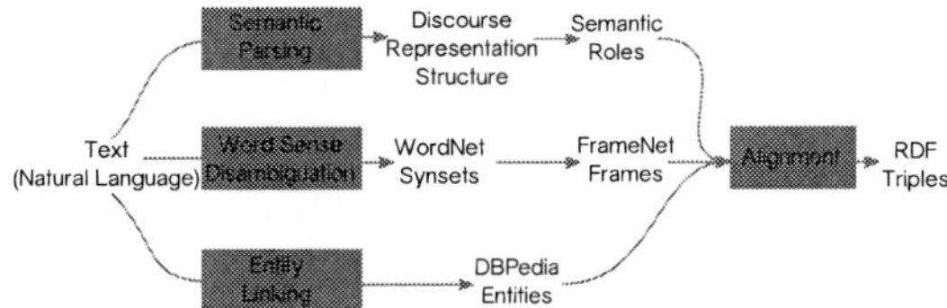

Figure 3: Architectural Scheme of KNEWS.

This pipeline is implemented in the KNEWS system, available for download at `https://github.com/valeriobasile/learningbyreading`. In the following paragraphs we describe the internal details of the components of KNEWS.

Semantic parsing   The semantic parsing module employs the C&C tools and Boxer to process the input text and output a complete formal representation of its meaning. The C&C pipeline of statistical NLP tools includes a tokenizer, a lemmatizer, named entity and part-of-speech tagger, and a parser that creates a Combinatorial Caregorial Grammar representation of the natural language syntax. Boxer builds a DRS on top of the CCG analysis. The predicates of a DRS are expressed over a set of *discourse referents* representing entities, concepts and events. Such structures contain, among other information, predicates representing the roles of the entities with respect to the detected events, e.g., event(A), entity(B), agent(A,B) to represent B playing the role of the *agent* of the event A.

Word sense disambiguation and Entity Linking KNEWS uses WordNet to represent concepts and events, DBpedia for named entities, and FrameNet's frames to represent events, integrating the mapping with the WordNet synsets provided by FrameBase. The inventory of thematic roles used by Boxer is taken from VerbNet (Schuler, 2005), while KNEWS employs the mapping provided by SemLinks (Palmer, 2009) to link them (whenever possible) to FrameNet roles. KNEWS can be configured to use either UKB (Agirre and Soroa, 2009) or Babelfy (Moro et al., 2014) to perform the word sense disambiguation, and DBpedia Spotlight (Daiber et al., 2013) or Babelfy for entity linking.

Output modes KNEWS's default output consists of frame instances, sets of RDF triples that contain a unique identifier, the type of the frame, the thematic roles involved in the instance, and the concepts or entities that fill the roles. The format follows the scheme of FrameBase, which offers the advantage of interoperability with other resources in the Linked Open Data cloud, as well as the possibility of using FrameBase's (de)reification rules to automatically generate a large number of binary predicates. An example of frame instance, extracted from the sentence "A robot is driving the car." is given in Figure 4.
This output mode of KNEWS has been employed in Basile et al. (2016) to create a repository of general knowledge about objects.

For the purpose of NLG, we extended KNEWS with a new output mode, similar to the previous one (frame instances) with the difference that it contains as additional information the alignment

with the text. We exploit the DRG output of Boxer to link the discourse referents to surface forms, i.e., span of the original input text, resulting in the word-aligned representation shown in Figure 5. This new output mode of KNEWS consist of an XML list of *frameinstance* elements. Each frame instance is equipped with its complete lexicalization (the *instancelexicalization* tag), the incomplete surface form associated with the event (the *framelexicalization* tag) and a sequence of *frameelements*. A *frameelement* represent a role in the frame instance. The *concept* tag contains a DBpedia or Wordnet resource (depending on the output of the disambiguation module), a lexicalization of the role filler (the *conceptlexicalization* tag), and the incomplete surface form obtained by composing the surface forms of the role filler and the frame. In the next section we describe an automatically built resource created by parsing text with this configuration of KNEWS.

KNEWS has also an additional output mode: First-order Logic. With this output mode, KNEWS is able to generate first-order logic formulae representing the natural language text given as input. The symbols for the predicates are Wordnet symbols, allowing the output of KNEWS to be integrated with a reasoning engine, e.g., to select background knowledge in a much more focused manner, as proposed in Furbach and Schon (2016).

5   Evaluation

In order to test our approach to knowledge extraction, we parsed a corpus of short texts, taken from the ESL Yes website of material for English learners.[2] We find this data particularly apt in the more general context of extracting general knowledge from text, being made of short, clear sentences about simple and generic topics. The corpus comprises 725 short stories, that we divided into 14,140 sentences. Parsing the ESL Yes corpus with KNEWS we collected 30,217 frame instances (420 unique frames), 1,455 concepts (1,201 WordNet synsets and 254 DBpedia entities) filling in 41,945 roles (161 unique roles). 29,409 role instances could not be mapped to FrameNet, so they are expressed by one of 18 VerbNet roles.

We evaluate the information extraction methodology by assessing the quality of this automatically produced resource. For each frame instance,

----

[2]http://www.eslyes.com/

```
@prefix rdf: <http://www.w3.org/1999/02/22-rdf-syntax-ns#> .
@prefix fb:  <http://framebase.org/ns/> .
@prefix dbr: <http://dbpedia.org/resource/> .
@prefix wn:  <http://wordnet-rdf.princeton.edu/wn31/> .

fb:fi-Operate_vehicle_dc59afa6 rdf:type fb:frame-Operate_vehicle-drive.v .
fb:fi-Operate_vehicle_dc59afa6 fb:fe-Driver dbr:Robot .
fb:fi-Operate_vehicle_dc59afa6 fb:fe-Vehicle wn:02961779-n .
```

Figure 4: RDF triples extracted by KNEWS from the sentence "A robot is driving the car", constituting one frame instance.

```
<frameinstance id=''Operate_vehicle_dc59afa6''
    type=''Operate_vehicle-drive.v'' internalvariable=''e1''>
  <framelexicalization>k3:x1 is driving k3:x2</framelexicalization>
  <instancelexicalization>The robot is driving the car .</instancelexicalization>
  <frameelements>
    <frameelement role=''Driver'' internalvariable=''x1''>
      <concept>http://dbpedia.org/resource/Robot</concept>
      <rolelexicalization>The robot is driving x2</roleexicalization>
      <conceptlexicalization>The robot</conceptlexicalization>
    </frameelement>
    <frameelement role=''Vehicle'' internalvariable=''x2''>
      <concept>http://wordnet-rdf.princeton.edu/wn31/02961779-n</concept>
      <rolelexicalization>x1 is driving the car .</roleexicalization>
      <conceptlexicalization>the car .</conceptlexicalization>
    </frameelement>
  </frameelements>
</frameinstance>
```

Figure 5: XML output of KNEWS describing a frame instance extracted from the sentence "A robot is driving the car".

if all the information is present and complete, it should be possible to recreate the instance lexicalization by applying the composition method of Basile and Bos (2013). The incomplete surface forms corresponding to the frame and the frame elements are automatically composed and compared to the original frame lexicalization. We ran this evaluation procedure on the resource and found 7,366 instances are correctly regenerated, that is, about one in four instances. Of the remaining instances, 11,996 present incorrect instance lexicalizations, usually containing variables instead of being complete surface forms. These occurrences are caused by misalignments in the representation produced by Boxer, so that the composition algorithm cannot recreate the original surface form. For instance, for the sentence "The mother gave her baby a red apple", the lexicalized DRG produced by Boxer, when the composition algorithm is applied to it, produces "The mother gave k5:x3 baby k4:x2". We also found that in 5,211 cases the presence subordination prevents the realization algorithm from working correctly, because no lexicalization is found for the discourse referent corresponding to the subordinate clause. In 1,865 cases, issues are caused by the presence of phrasal verbs (e.g. "He picked up his clothes") or adverbs, which are analyzed by Boxer using the

Table 1: Error analysis of the automatically produced, text-aligned frame instance collection, broken down by number of frame elements.

roles	1	2	3	all
correct	4,774	2,374	218	7,366
subordination	4,824	368	19	5,211
adverb	1,288	561	16	1,865
realization	5,885	5,508	603	11,996
other	2,672	1,009	98	3,779
total	19,443	9,820	954	30,217

relation *manner* between the event and the adverb or proposition, thus like in the previous case no lexicalization is found for all the discourse referents. Finally, 3,779 instances failed the test due to a variety of reasons, e.g., failure of the entity linking module or wrong syntactic analysis. Table 1 summarizes the findings exposed so far, also broken down by the number of frame elements in the frame instances.

When increasing number of frame elements per frame instance, the issues with subordinate constructions dramatically decreases: they amount to 24% of the cases with one frame elements, 3% and 1% with two and three frame elements respectively. Conversely, wrong realizations due to representation misalignments tends to get worse, involving from 30% of the instances with one frame elements to 56% with two, to 39% with three.

6 Generation of Frame Lexicalizations

The first and most obvious use for the resource presented here in the context of NLG is given by the set of lexicalizations it provides for concepts and entities. In the example in Figure 5, for instance, the DBpedia entity `Robot` is lexicalized as "A robot" and the synset `02961779-n` as "the car". Moreover, the frame is also given the lexicalization with two open variables "x_1 is driving x_2". Indeed, the surface forms provided by the DRG can be *incomplete*, that is, containing variables that can be used to compose a full surface form from the single ones corresponding to the discourse referents, e.g., x_1:"A robot" and e_1:"x_1 is driving x_2" compose to form e_1:"A robot is driving x_2", and so on.

This composition mechanism gives us the opportunity to devise a simple method to produce new frame lexicalizations. Given new concepts or entities with the respective lexicalizations and roles (e.g., Driver: "Valentino Rossi", Vehicule: "the motorbike"), they can be replaced in the appropriate frame instance so that the variables x_1 and x_2 are linked respectively to "Valentino Rossi" and "the motorbike". A subsequent step of composition will then yield the new frame lexicalization "Valentino Rossi is driving the motorbike".

We developed a simple prototype in order to test this approach to NLG from frame instances. This prototype is based on the resource described in Section 5, restricted to the instances with exactly two frame elements and associated with a complete surface form. The procedure we use to evaluate the system is the following:

1. For each frame instance, produce four new frame instances by replacing one or both frame elements, either with similar concepts or with randomly chosen concepts.

2. Generate the lexicalization of the new frames by composing the frame lexicalization structure with the new concept lexicalizations.

3. For each of the four scenarios, select randomly one hundred instance lexicalization for the evaluation.

4. Manually inspect the selected lexicalizations according to three possible classes of fluency: *nonsensical* (the sentence is not grammatical and it does not make sense), *informative*

Table 2: Result of the manual evaluation of the NLG prototype based on the collection of lexicalized frame instances.

Replaced frame elements	Judgment nonsensical/informative/fluent
1, most similar	23/33/44
2, most similar	24/53/23
1, random	23/35/42
2, random	54/23/23

(the grammar contains mistakes but the information is clearly transmitted), and *fluent* (the lexicalization correctly conveys the input knowledge).

When we replace one frame element or both of them with similar concepts, we rely on the WUP similarity defined by Wu and Palmer (1994) for pairs of WordNet synsets, a measure of path distance weighted according to the depth of the WordNet taxonomy. We compute the WUP similarity for each pair of concepts in our colelction and replace one or both frame elements with their most similar concepts. For example, the frame elements corresponding to the *Vehicle* in the frame instance in Figure 5 is associated with the concept `http://wordnet-rdf.princeton.edu/wn31/02961779-n` (car, automobile). This concept could be replaced, for the sake of the evaluation, by the similar concept (according to the WUP metric) `http://wordnet-rdf.princeton.edu/wn31/104497386-n` (truck), if this is also in the collection. A new lexicalization is then produced by composition "A robot is driving **the truck**". The lexicalization for the replaced concepts is chosen as the most frequent lexicalization of that particular concept, to minimize the occuprrence of awkward realizations like "A robot is driving **of the truck**".

Note that we only judge fluency. An evaluation of adequacy or other content-oriented metrics should also take into account the input and would be more difficult to evaluate in this setting, since here the input is artificially produced by replacing elements of the frame instances.

The manual inspection of the produced frame instance lexicalizations resulted in the figures shown in Table 2. As expected, replacing both frame elements instead of just one leads to more errors in the realizations. This problem can be mitigated by increasing the coverage of the resource. With a larger collection, the chance of retrieving a frame instance with at least one frame element in common with the new input is higher, thus there will be more cases where only one frame element is new. Interestingly, the choice of concepts to generate with respect to the frame (similar vs. random) does not seem to influence the outcome. The result of this pilot study are encouraging in that a sufficiently large number of correct realizations are produced by a simple mechanism. However, a more thourough evaluation is needed, especially with respect to the coverage (and thus the scalability) of our approach.

7 Conclusion and Future Work

In this paper we introduced a novel methodology to extract knowledge from text and encode it in formal structures compatible with the standards of the Web. Such structures are essentially instances of frames with their frame elements linked to concepts in Wordnet or DBpedia. This methodology is implemented in the freely available software package KNEWS. Next, we presented a collection of frame instances aligned with natural language, automatically created by parsing text for English learners. Finally, we propose a pilot study on how to use this resource to generate natural language from new frame instances.

In terms of future direction for this work, the low hanging fruit is the enlargement of the resource, which will lead to a higher number of "good" instances to use for direct generation (as shown in Section 6) and more data to use for a statistical approach to generation. Since the resource is produced automatically by parsing raw text with KNEWS, and natural language is abundant on the Web, this is a direction we intend to take in the foreseeable future.

The approach to NLG based on the collection of lexicalized frame instances introduced in NLG is at the preliminary work stage, and many refinements can be made to the algorithm. Given a new frame instance to generate, its frame elements could be matched to the lexicalization in the resource with more sophisticated methods, e.g., using distributional similarity.

As a possible extension to the resource, information such as lemma and number could be included in the lexicalization of concepts. With such information in place, the NLG algorithm could be interfaced with the SimpleNLG surface realization library (Gatt and Reiter, 2009) to produce more fluent lexicalizations.

The main selling point of a large knowledge base aligned with text is that its size allows researchers to develop statistical methods to learn a mapping between the formaly encoded knowledge and natural language. While this could be a very challenging enterprise, as highlighted by the work presented in Basile (2015), this work of constitutes a first step in this direction.

References

Eneko Agirre and Aitor Soroa. 2009. Personalizing pagerank for word sense disambiguation. In *Proceedings of the 12th Conference of the European Chapter of the Association for Computational Linguistics*, EACL '09, pages 33–41, Stroudsburg, PA, USA. Association for Computational Linguistics.

Collin F. Baker, Charles J. Fillmore, and John B. Lowe. 1998. The berkeley framenet project. In *Proceedings of the 17th International Conference on Computational Linguistics - Volume 1*, COLING '98, pages 86–90, Stroudsburg, PA, USA. Association for Computational Linguistics.

Valerio Basile and Johan Bos. 2013. Aligning Formal Meaning Representations with Surface Strings for Wide-coverage Text Generation. In *ENLG 2013*, page 1.

Valerio Basile, Johan Bos, Kilian Evang, and Noortje Venhuizen. 2012. Developing a large semantically annotated corpus. In *Proceedings of the Eighth International Conference on Language Resources and Evaluation (LREC 2012)*, pages 3196–3200, Istanbul, Turkey.

Valerio Basile, Elena Cabrio, and Fabien Gandon. 2016. Building a general knowledge base of physical objects for robots. In *The Semantic Web. Latest Advances and New Domains*.

Valerio Basile. 2014. A lesk-inspired unsupervised algorithm for lexical choice from wordnet synsets. *The First Italian Conference on Computational Linguistics CLiC-it 2014*, page 48.

Valerio Basile. 2015. *From logic to language: Natural language generation from logical forms.* Ph.D. thesis.

Anja Belz, Michael White, Dominic Espinosa, Eric Kow, Deirdre Hogan, and Amanda Stent. 2011. The first surface realisation shared task: Overview and evaluation results. In *Proceedings of the 13th European Workshop on Natural Language Generation*, ENLG '11, pages 217–226, Stroudsburg, PA, USA. Association for Computational Linguistics.

Johan Bos. 2008. Wide-coverage semantic analysis with boxer. In *Semantics in Text Processing. STEP 2008 Conference Proceedings*, volume 1, pages 277–286.

Nadjet Bouayad-Agha, Gerard Casamayor, Simon Mille, Marco Rospocher, Horacio Saggion, Luciano Serafini, and Leo Wanner. 2012. From ontology to nl: Generation of multilingual user-oriented environmental reports. In Gosse Bouma, Ashwin Ittoo, Elisabeth Métais, and Hans Wortmann, editors, *Natural Language Processing and Information Systems*, volume 7337 of *Lecture Notes in Computer Science*, pages 216–221. Springer Berlin Heidelberg.

Aoife Cahill and Josef Van Genabith. 2006. Robust pcfg-based generation using automatically acquired lfg approximations. In *In Proceedings of the 44th ACL*.

James R. Curran, Stephen Clark, and Johan Bos. 2007. Linguistically motivated large-scale nlp with c&c and boxer. In *Proceedings of the 45th Annual Meeting of the ACL on Interactive Poster and Demonstration Sessions*, ACL '07, pages 33–36, Stroudsburg, PA, USA. Association for Computational Linguistics.

Joachim Daiber, Max Jakob, Chris Hokamp, and Pablo N. Mendes. 2013. Improving efficiency and accuracy in multilingual entity extraction. In *Proceedings of the 9th International Conference on Semantic Systems (I-Semantics)*.

Charles Fillmore. 1982. Frame semantics. *Linguistics in the morning calm*, pages 111–137.

Ulrich Furbach and Claudia Schon. 2016. Commonsense reasoning meets theorem proving. In *Proceedings of Workshop on Bridging the Gap between Human and Automated Reasoning*.

Albert Gatt and Ehud Reiter. 2009. Simplenlg: A realisation engine for practical applications. In *Proceedings of the 12th European Workshop on Natural Language Generation*, ENLG '09, pages 90–93, Stroudsburg, PA, USA. Association for Computational Linguistics.

Bikash Gyawali and Claire Gardent. 2014. Surface realisation from knowledge-bases. In *Proceedings of the 52nd Annual Meeting of the Association for Computational Linguistics (Volume 1: Long Papers)*, pages 424–434, Baltimore, Maryland, June. Association for Computational Linguistics.

Julia Hockenmaier and Mark Steedman. 2007. Ccgbank: A corpus of ccg derivations and dependency structures extracted from the penn treebank. *Comput. Linguist.*, 33(3):355–396, September.

Hongyan Jing. 1998. Usage of wordnet in natural language generation. In *Proceedings of the Joint 17th International Conference on Computational Linguistics 36th Annual Meeting of the Association for Computational Linguistics (COLING-ACL'98) workshop on Usage of WordNet in Natural Language Processing Systems*, pages 128–134.

Hans Kamp and Uwe Reyle. 1993. *From Discourse to Logic. Introduction to Modeltheoretic Semantics of Natural Language, Formal Logic and Discourse Representation Theory*. Kluwer, Dordrecht.

Edward Loper, Szu ting Yi, and Martha Palmer. 2007. Combining lexical resources: Mapping between propbank and verbnet. In *In Proceedings of the 7th International Workshop on Computational Linguistics*.

Mitchell P. Marcus, Beatrice Santorini, and Mary Ann Marcinkiewicz. 1993. Building a large annotated corpus of english: The penn treebank. *COMPUTATIONAL LINGUISTICS*, 19(2):313–330.

George A. Miller. 1995. Wordnet: A lexical database for english. *Commun. ACM*, 38(11):39–41, November.

Andrea Moro, Alessandro Raganato, and Roberto Navigli. 2014. Entity Linking meets Word Sense Disambiguation: a Unified Approach. *Transactions of the Association for Computational Linguistics (TACL)*, 2:231–244.

Martha. Palmer. 2009. SemLink: Linking PropBank, VerbNet and FrameNet. In *Proceedings of the Generative Lexicon Conference*, Pisa, Italy, Sept.

Jacobo Rouces, Gerard de Melo, and Katja Hose. 2015. Framebase: Representing n-ary relations using semantic frames. In Fabien Gandon, Marta Sabou, Harald Sack, Claudia d'Amato, Philippe Cudr-Mauroux, and Antoine Zimmermann, editors, *ESWC*, volume 9088 of *Lecture Notes in Computer Science*, pages 505–521. Springer.

Karin Kipper Schuler. 2005. *Verbnet: A Broadcoverage, Comprehensive Verb Lexicon*. Ph.D. thesis, Philadelphia, PA, USA. AAI3179808.

Mihai Surdeanu, Richard Johansson, Adam Meyers, Lluís Màrquez, and Joakim Nivre. 2008. The conll-2008 shared task on joint parsing of syntactic and semantic dependencies. In *Proceedings of the Twelfth Conference on Computational Natural Language Learning*, CoNLL '08, pages 159–177, Stroudsburg, PA, USA. Association for Computational Linguistics.

Michael White, Rajakrishnan Rajkumar, and Scott Martin. 2007. Towards broad coverage surface realization with ccg. In *In Proc. of the Workshop on Using Corpora for NLG: Language Generation and Machine Translation (UCNLG+MT*.

Zhibiao Wu and Martha Palmer. 1994. Verbs semantics and lexical selection. In *Proceedings of the 32Nd Annual Meeting on Association for Computational Linguistics*, ACL '94, pages 133–138, Stroudsburg, PA, USA. Association for Computational Linguistics.

Processing Document Collections to Automatically Extract Linked Data: Semantic Storytelling Technologies for Smart Curation Workflows

Peter Bourgonje, Julian Moreno Schneider, Georg Rehm, Felix Sasaki
DFKI GmbH, Language Technology Lab
Alt-Moabit 91c,
10559 Berlin, Germany
{peter.bourgonje, julian.moreno_schneider, georg.rehm,
felix.sasaki}@dfki.de

Abstract

We develop a system that operates on a document collection and represents the contained information to enable the intuitive and efficient exploration of the collection. Using various NLP, IE and Semantic Web methods, we generate a semantic layer on top of the collection, from which we take the key concepts. We define templates for structured reorganisation and rearrange the information related to the key concepts to fit the respective template. The use case of the system is to support knowledge workers (journalists, editors, curators, etc.) in their task of processing large amounts of documents by summarising the information contained in these documents and suggesting potential story paths that the knowledge worker can then process further.

1 Introduction and Context

Journalists writing a story typically have access to large databases that contain information relevant to their topic. Due to the novelty requirement, they are under pressure to produce a story in a short amount of time. They have to provide relevant background, but also present information that is new and eye-opening. Curators who design showrooms or museum exhibitions often cannot afford to spend much time on getting familiar with a new domain, due to the large variety of unrelated domains they work in. Several other job profiles rely on extracting key concepts from a large document collection on a specific domain and understanding how they are related to one another. We refer to the group of people facing this challenge as *knowledge workers*. The common ground of their tasks is the *curation of digital information*. In our two-year project we collaborate with four SME partner companies that cover four different use cases and sectors (Rehm and Sasaki, 2015). We develop technologies that enable knowledge workers to

delegate routine tasks to the machine so that they can concentrate on their core task, i. e., producing a story that is based on a specific genre or text type and that relies on facts contained in a document collection. Among the tools that we develop and integrate into the emerging platform are semantic storytelling, named entity recognition, entity linking, temporal analysis, machine translation, summarisation, classification and clustering. We currently focus on making available RESTful APIs to our SME partners that provide basic functionalities that can be integrated into their own in-house systems. In addition, we work on implementing a system for semantic storytelling. This system will process large document collections, extract entities and relations between them, extract temporal information and events in order to automatically produce a hypertext view of the collection to enable knowledge workers to familiarise themselves with the document collection in a fast and efficient way. We also experiment with automatically generating story paths through this hypertext cluster that can then be used as the foundation of a new piece of content. The focus of this paper is on the approach we use to fill templates that assist the user in the generation of a story and on selecting possible topics for a new story.

2 Related Work

The emerging platform we develop connects all RESTful APIs that perform the individual analyses by using the FREME framework (Sasaki et al., 2015) throughout. A system with a similar setup is described in (Lewis et al., 2014), but unlike our platform, this is mainly targeted at the localisation industry and it deploys a different approach to representing curated data. Other systems aimed at collecting and processing semantically enriched content are developed in the context

Proceedings of the 2nd International Workshop on Natural Language Generation and the Semantic Web (WebNLG), pages 13–16,
Edinburgh, Scotland, September 6th, 2016. ©2016 Association for Computational Linguistics

of the NewsReader project [1], specifically targeted at the news domain and the SUMMA project [2], focusing on broad coverage of languages through the use of machine translation. Our approach towards language generation consists of filling templates to create building blocks for a story (which are not grammatical sentences), and it deviates from a.o. (Cimiano et al., 2013), (Galanis and Androutsopoulos, 2007), (Bontcheva and Wilks, 2004) in that it does not focus on one specific domain and it includes collecting the information that goes into the ontology. Our approach is based on extracting relations between entities. Because of our focus on domain adaptability, we plan to avoid the labour-intensive selection of seed patterns that comes with (semi-)supervised approaches as described in (Xu et al., 2013), (Brin, 1998), (Agichtein and Gravano, 2000) and (Etzioni et al., 2005). We use an unsupervised approach instead with an open set of relation types. A similar system is described in (Yates et al., 2007). For ease of integration reasons we implement an in-house approach to relation extract, as described in 4.

3   Linked Data Generation

We produce a semantic layer over the document collection consisting of a set of annotations for every document, represented in NIF[3]. Frequent named entities are interpreted as key concepts. An essential step in producing the semantic layer is therefore the spotting and linking of named entities. One of our APIs performs entity spotting based on pre-trained sample models (Nothman et al., 2012) and linking based on DBPedia Spotlight [4]. Because the users of our tools work on a variety of specific domains, the platform provides the possibility to train a model or to plug in a domain-specific ontology and upload a key-value structured dictionary. The NER module is based on the corresponding Apache OpenNLP module (Apache Software Foundation, 2016). The NER API generates a NIF representation of the input in which every recognised entity is annotated with the corresponding URI in DBPedia. Specialised

SPARQL queries are used to retrieve type-specific related information (like birth and death dates and places for persons, geo-coordinates for locations, etc.). This information is added to the semantic layer and is used to fill particular slots in our story templates.

4   Semantic Storytelling

For the task of storytelling we use a template-filling approach. The user selects one or more concepts and one or more templates that we attempt to fill using the semantic layer. We have defined a *biography* template and an *event* template. The biography template contains the following slots: full name, pseudonym, date of birth, place of birth, date of death, place of death, mother, father, siblings, spouse, children, occupation, key persons and key locations. The event template contains slots for date(s), key persons and key locations. To collect the information needed to fill the individual slots in the templates, the results of the type-specific SPARQL queries are used. Information in the ontology is typically of higher quality than information extracted using a relation extraction component. However, because the user often works in domains for which no ontology is available, relation extraction is used to search for the missing information in the document collection. In addition to filling slots in templates, the output of relation extraction between entities allows the user to learn about relations between key concepts that are not directly related to any slots in the templates. This allows the user to get a better understanding of the document collection, but can also be the basis for selecting and populating a new event template, hence generating an angle for a new story. Relations are extracted in the following way: A document collection is assumed to be relatively homogeneous from a content perspective (file types and information type (running text or metadata) may vary, but the information in a collection is assumed to be about one domain). The goal is to aggregate information and extract relevant relations regardless of which document these originate from. The assumption is that in the NER procedure all relevant concepts have been annotated and are present in the semantic layer. For every sentence containing two or more entities, a dependency tree is generated using the Stanford CoreNLP DependencyParser (Manning

---

[1]http://www.newsreader-project.eu/

[2]http://www.summa-project.eu/

[3]See   http://persistence.uni-leipzig.org/nlp2rdf/ontologies/nif-core/nif-core.html

[4]https://github.com/dkt-projekt/e-NLP contains code and documentation

et al., 2014). The entities are located in the tree, and a relation between entity A and entity B is established if A has a subject-type dependency relation to a verb node in the dependency graph and B has an object-type dependency relation to this same verb node in the graph. The value of this verb node (e.g. the token) is taken to express the relation. For collecting missing information related to specific slots in the template we plan to include a dedicated relation extraction system and train it with a number of seeds that correspond directly to the slots in the template we want to fill. Because of the limited number of relation types that are needed for this, a (semi-)supervised, seed-based approach is likely to produce useful results. For selecting new angles for a story (in the form of events as the basis for a new template), we want to capture a larger set of relation types. Since the domain typically determines the predominant relation types present in a collection, this calls for a more open approach that is not limited by the relation types covered by the seeds. To give an idea of the current stage of our relation extraction component, a demo-interface based on the Viking corpus is available at: `http://dev.digitale-kuratierung. de/ds/selectstory.php`.

5 Evaluation

To assess the suitability of the platform for the tasks of template filling and interactive collection exploration, we have asked four humans to perform these tasks and in the process evaluate the platform. For evaluation, three collections were used, two of them real-world use-cases provided by the SME partners of the project: (i) a collection of letters sent by the architect Erich Mendelsohn and his wife [5] and (ii) a private document collection on Vikings. The third collection is the Wiki-Wars corpus [6].

The subjects were asked to check how many slots in the templates could be filled with the relations extracted. For the biography template some relevant relations were found in the Viking corpus: *Edward, marry, Edith*, which can fill the spouse slot and *William, raise, Malcolm*, which could fill the children slot (though it of course does not imply that Malcolm really is a child of William). Be-

cause we have not created a gold standard from these corpora, measuring recall is problematic. As a result, it is not clear whether the approach failed to extract the relations that could lead to populating templates, or whether this information was not present in the corpus. It is clear however that the real-world scenario would primarily rely on getting information from the ontology. An observation that was made by all test subjects was that the quality of the relations extracted from the WikiWars and the Viking corpus was much higher than that of relations extracted from the Mendelsohn corpus. This is probably due to the fact that the first two corpora are meant to be descriptive and clear records of historical events, whereas the Mendelsohn corpus consists of private letters that were probably not intended to be descriptive for the general public. In addition, the Mendelsohn letters contained many cases of *you* and *I*, which were not recognized by the NER component (because resolution to a URI is not in all cases straightforward), hence these sentences were not considered. With regard to the task of exploring the document collection and selecting possible events to base a new story on, the subjects reported that several useful relations were extracted, again with the exception of the Mendelsohn corpus. Examples are *[William [[extort, Harold], [leave, Aldred]]]* from the Viking corpus and *[Rome, annex, [Sardinia, Corsica]]* and *[Tripartite pact, unite, [Italy, Germany, Japan]]* from the WikiWars corpus. These pieces of information also display the advantage of a non-seed-based approach. To capture the above relations, we would need to have trained for relations of the extort-, leave-, annex- and unite-type. The point however is that upfront the potentially interesting relations that need to be extracted are of unknown types.

A drawback of the current approach is the fact that only binary relations (a predicate with two arguments) are extracted. Ditransitive verbs are not fully captured. Instead, we end up with relations like *[Edward, give, William]*, where an important piece of the expressed relation is missing. Another drawback is the requirement that the two entities are connected through the same verb node in the dependency graph. We have no concrete figures on recall, but the number of extracted relations were relatively low for all corpora. A third observed issue were errors introduced by the dependency parser. Relations like *[United States, mem-*

---

[5] `http://ema.smb.museum/en/home/`
[6] `http://timexportal. wikidot.com/forum/t-275092/ wikiwars-is-available-for-download`

ber, Allies] and *[Poland, better, Russian Empire]* were extracted, where apparently *member* and *better* were tagged as a verb, hence considered by our analysis.

6 Conclusion

We present a platform that generates a semantic layer over a document collection and applies relation extraction to fill templates that serve as building blocks for the generation of new stories. This information is extracted, analysed, in some cases rearranged and presented to the user in the form of (i) filled out templates or (ii) through an interactive tree-based exploratory view. Test users pointed out its usefulness to exploring the contents of a collection in a fast and intuitive way and its shortcomings with regard to non-binary relations, low recall and lack of parsing precision. The most important suggestions for future work are looking into means of extracting indirect objects (or generally relevant additional information for specific relations, such as location or time) and defining paths through the dependency graphs rather than requiring direct connections in the graph. In addition we plan to plug in a verb ontology to be able to group the different types of relations we find.

References

Eugene Agichtein and Luis Gravano. 2000. Snowball: Extracting relations from large plain-text collections. In *Proceedings of the Fifth ACM Conference on Digital Libraries*, DL '00, pages 85–94, New York, NY, USA. ACM.

Apache Software Foundation. 2016. Apache OpenNLP, http://opennlp.apache.org.

Kalina Bontcheva and Yorick Wilks. 2004. Automatic report generation from ontologies: The MIAKT approach. In Farid Meziane and Elisabeth Métais, editors, *Natural Language Processing and Information Systems, 9th International Conference on Applications of Natural Languages to Information Systems, NLDB 2004, Salford, UK, June 23-25, 2004, Proceedings*, volume 3136 of *Lecture Notes in Computer Science*, pages 324–335. Springer.

Sergey Brin. 1998. Extracting patterns and relations from the world wide web. In *In WebDB Workshop at 6th International Conference on Extending Database Technology, EDBT98*, pages 172–183.

Philipp Cimiano, Janna Lüker, David Nagel, and Christina Unger. 2013. Exploiting ontology lexica for generating natural language texts from rdf data. In *Proceedings of the 14th European Workshop on Natural Language Generation*, pages 10–19, Sofia, Bulgaria, August. Association for Computational Linguistics.

Oren Etzioni, Michael Cafarella, Doug Downey, Ana Maria Popescu, Tal Shaked, Stephen Soderland, Daniel S. Weld, and Alexander Yates. 2005. Unsupervised named-entity extraction from the web: An experimental study. *Artificial Intelligence*, 165(1):91–134, 6.

D. Galanis and I. Androutsopoulos. 2007. Generating Multilingual Descriptions from Linguistically Annotated OWL Ontologies: the NaturalOWL System. In *Proceedings of the 11th European Workshop on Natural Language Generation (ENLG 2007)*, pages 143–146, Schloss Dagstuhl, Germany.

David Lewis, Asunción Gómez-Pérez, Sebastian Hellman, and Felix Sasaki. 2014. The role of linked data for content annotation and translation. In *Proceedings of the 2014 European Data Forum*, EDF '14.

Christopher D. Manning, Mihai Surdeanu, John Bauer, Jenny Finkel, Steven J. Bethard, and David McClosky. 2014. The Stanford CoreNLP natural language processing toolkit. In *Association for Computational Linguistics (ACL) System Demonstrations*, pages 55–60.

Joel Nothman, Nicky Ringland, Will Radford, Tara Murphy, and James R. Curran. 2012. Learning multilingual named entity recognition from Wikipedia. *Artificial Intelligence*, 194:151–175.

Georg Rehm and Felix Sasaki. 2015. Digitale Kuratierungstechnologien – Verfahren für die effiziente Verarbeitung, Erstellung und Verteilung qualitativ hochwertiger Medieninhalte. In *Proceedings of the 2015 International Conference of the German Society for Computational Linguistics and Language Technology*, GSCL '15, pages 138–139.

Felix Sasaki, T. Gornostay, M. Dojchinovski, M. Osella, E. Mannens, G. Stoitsis, Philip Richie, T. Declerck, and Kevin Koidl. 2015. Introducing freme: Deploying linguistic linked data. In *Proceedings of the 4th Workshop of the Multilingual Semantic Web*, MSW '15.

Feiyu Xu, Hans Uszkoreit, Hong Li, Peter Adolphs, and Xiwen Cheng, 2013. *Domain Adaptive Relation Extraction for Semantic Web*, chapter X. Springer.

Alexander Yates, Michael Cafarella, Michele Banko, Oren Etzioni, Matthew Broadhead, and Stephen Soderland. 2007. Textrunner: Open information extraction on the web. In *Proceedings of Human Language Technologies: The Annual Conference of the North American Chapter of the Association for Computational Linguistics: Demonstrations*, NAACL-Demonstrations '07, pages 25–26, Stroudsburg, PA, USA. Association for Computational Linguistics.

On the Robustness of Standalone Referring Expression Generation Algorithms Using RDF Data

Pablo Ariel Duboue and **Martin Ariel Domínguez** and **Paula Estrella**
Facultad de Matematica, Astronomía y Física
Universidad Nacional de Córdoba
Córdoba, Argentina

Abstract

A sub-task of Natural Language Generation (NLG) is the generation of referring expressions (REG). REG algorithms are expected to select attributes that unambiguously identify an entity with respect to a set of distractors. In previous work we have defined a methodology to evaluate REG algorithms using real life examples. In the present work, we evaluate REG algorithms using a dataset that contains alterations in the properties of referring entities. We found that naturally occurring ontological re-engineering can have a devastating impact in the performance of REG algorithms, with some more robust in the presence of these changes than others. The ultimate goal of this work is observing the behavior and estimating the performance of a series of REG algorithms as the entities in the data set evolve over time.

1 Introduction

The main research focus in NLG is the creation of computer systems capable of generating human-like language. According to the consensus Natural Language Generation (NLG) architecture (Cahill et al., 2001) the NLG task takes as input non-linguistic data and operates over it as a series of enrichment steps, culminating with fully specified sentences from which output strings can be read out. Such a generation pipeline mimics, up to a certain extent, a Natural Language Understanding (NLU) pipeline. In NLU, however, it is expected that the text upon which the system is being run upon might contain a variety of errors. These errors include wrongly written text that a human might find it difficult to understand or idiosyncratic deviations from well accepted prose (what is called "improper grammar" or "orthographic mistakes" by defenders of prescriptive grammar). The fact that plenty of texts of interest to NLU exhibit poor quality explains the reason behind NLU's focus on *robust* approaches. Such approaches attempt to cope gracefully with inputs that do not conform to the standards of the original texts employed for building the system (either as working examples or training data in a machine learning sense). In NLG, on the other hand, current approaches rarely explore fallback strategies for those cases where the data is not fully compliant with the expected input and, thus, there is little intuition about possible outputs of a system under such circumstances.

In this work we aim to explore robustness for the particular case of Referring Expressions Generation (REG) algorithms by means of different versions of an ontology. Therefore, we can combine REG algorithms with ontologies to study their behavior as the entities in the chosen ontology change. In our case, we have chosen the ontology built from Wikipedia though different versions of DBpedia and three REG algorithms on which we will measure robustness, defined here as an algorithm's resilience to adapt to changes in the data or its capability to gracefully deal with noisy data. In a sense, we are interested in two different phenomena: (1) whether an NLG subcomponent (REG in particular) can be used with outdated ontological data to fulfill its task and (2) which implementation of the said subcomponent is better suited in this setting. Our research is driven by the second question but this current work sheds more light on the first one. See Section 7 for details.

This paper is structured as follows: next section briefly mentions the relevant related work, in Section 3 and Section 4 we describe the algorithms applied and data used, respectively; in Section 5 we describe the setup used in the experiments, then

Proceedings of the 2nd International Workshop on Natural Language Generation and the Semantic Web (WebNLG), pages 17–24,
Edinburgh, Scotland, September 6th, 2016. ©2016 Association for Computational Linguistics

Section 6 presents the results which are further discussed in Section 7.

2 Related work

The need to account for changes in ontologies has long been acknowledged, given that they may not be useful in real world applications if the representation of the knowledge they contain is outdated. Eder and Koncilia (2004) present a formalism to represent ontologies as graphs that contain a time model including time intervals and valid times for concepts. They base their formalism on techniques developed for temporal databases, namely the versioning of databases instead of their evolution and they provide some guidelines on its possible implementation.

Another source of ontology transformation is spatiotemporal changes. Dealing with spatial changes on historical data (or over time series) is crucial for some NLP tasks, such as information retrieval (Kauppinen and Hyvnen, 2007). In their case, the authors deal with the evolution of the ontology's underlying domain instead of its versioning or evolution due to developments or refinements. Their main result is the definition of partial overlaps between concepts in a given time series, which was applied to build a Finnish Temporal Region Ontology, showing promising results.

More recently, with the development of one of the largest ontologies, DBpedia (Bizer et al., 2009), much research has been devoted to exploiting this resource in NLP or NLG tasks as well as to model its changes. For example, there is research on modeling DBpedia's currency (Rula et al., 2014), that is, the age of the data in it and the speed at which those changes can be captured by any system. Although currency could be computed based on the modification/creation dates of the resources, this information is not always present in Wikipedia pages. To overcome this, the authors propose a model to estimate currency combining information from the original related pages and a couple of currency metrics measuring the speed of retrieval by a system and basic currency or timestamp. Their experiments suggest that entities with high system currency are associated with more complete DBpedia resources and entities with low system currency appear associated with Wikipedia pages that are not easily tractable (or that "could not provide real world information" according with the authors).

Closer to our work, Kutlak et al. (2013) use DBpedia for REG. As opposed to classical work in the field, this work experiments with entities that potentially have a large number of distractors, a situation that may be difficult to handle for classical REG algorithms. Under this hypothesis, the authors propose a new corpus-based algorithm inspired by the notion of Communal Common Ground (CCG), defined as information shared by a particular community whose members assume that everyone knows. In the extrinsic evaluation CCG outperformed the more classical Incremental Algorithm (IA) (Dale and Reiter, 1995), thus authors suggest that CCG might be more suitable for large domains than other algorithms.

In previous work, we (Pacheco et al., 2012) employed several REG algorithms to generate referring expressions from DBpedia, in particular we used Full Brevity (Bohnet, 2007), Constraint Satisfaction approach (Gardent, 2002) and the Incremental Algorithm (Dale and Reiter, 1995). Exploiting articles from Wikinews to generate the RE for a randomly selected group of entities (a technique we also used in this work), we found that DBpedia contained information about half of the entities mentioned in the news and that the IA and the Constraint Satisfaction were able to generate a definite description in about 98% of the contexts extracted from the news articles. However, the algorithms produced satisfactory definite descriptions only in about 40% of the cases. The main problems identified in these experiments were that some properties are quite unique but lead to descriptions of little use to most people evaluating them (thus producing the low results obtained) and the rather odd choice of the preference order of the Incremental Algorithm. Our focus on robustness, however, is different from it.

In an earlier version of this work (Duboue et al., 2015), we analyzed only people rather than people and organizations and had an experimental mishap where the old version included tuples from the new version of DBpedia, producing results that were too optimistic. Even with the issue with the previous results, it encouraged us to use robustness as a metric for learning the IA ordering, an intriguing idea we explored recently, with mixed results (Duboue and Domínguez, 2016).

3 Algorithms

In this section we describe the REG algorithms used in this work. We chose three representative algorithms that can deal with single entity referents, a classic algorithm (Dale and Reiter, 1995), an algorithm generating negations (Gardent, 2002) and an algorithm using graph theory (Krahmer et al., 2003). We describe each of the algorithms using the following notation: R is the referent, C is the set of distractors and P is a list of properties, triples in the form (entity, attribute, value), describing R.

REG algorithms pick properties that might ultimately be used to generate nominal syntactic units that identify the entity that is the referent.[1] We define the context as the set of entities that the receiver is currently paying attention to. Then, the distractor set is the context set without the predicted reference. Once this is defined, they consider the components of a referral expression as rules to set aside or keep on considering the members of the contrast set. For example, if the speaker wants to identify a *small black dog* in a situation where the distractor set consists of a *big white dog* and a *black small cat*, we could choose the adjective black to rule out the white dog and then the noun dog to rule out the noun cat. The resulting referral expression would be the black dog, which refers to R but not to the other entities in this context. Thus, the R was unmistakably identified.

The algorithms listed here are implemented in the Java programming language and publicly available under an Open Source license as part of the Alusivo REG project.[2]

3.1 Incremental Algorithm

The incremental algorithm assumes the properties in P are ordered according to an established criteria. Then the algorithm iterates over P, adding each triple one at a time and removing from C all entities ruled out by the new triple. Triples that do not eliminate any new entity from C are ignored. The algorithm terminates when C is empty. This algorithm was created in 1995 (Dale and Reiter,

1995) as a simplification of previous work on the development of REG algorithms. Given its simplicity it is considered a baseline in many NLG articles.

This algorithm is strongly influenced by the preference order among attributes. We used the ordering for people in Wikipedia developed by Pacheco (Pacheco, 2012) which is shipped with Alusivo.

3.2 Gardent Algorithm

The algorithm (Gardent, 2002) is based on the idea that in many languages, a possible way to unambiguously describe entities is to identify a set of related referents and to provide a quantified expression, for example, *"the team where Messi has played that is not in Argentina"* should suffice to identify *Barcelona Ftbol Club* as the referred entity. The speaker offers enough information to the listener to identify the set of objects the speaker is talking about. From a generation perspective, this means that starting with a set of objects and their properties which are known to the speaker and the listener, a distinctive description must be created, in such a way that it allows the user to unmistakably identify the referred objects. The solution addressed from this standpoint is an algorithm that generates minimal distinct descriptions, that is to say, with the least number of literals to identify the target. By definition, these will not be unnecessarily long, redundant nor ambiguous. The algorithm performs this task using Constraint Satisfaction Programming (CSP) (Lassez, 1987)[3] to solve two basic constraints: find a set of positive properties P^+ and negative properties P^-, such that all properties in P^+ are true for the referent and all in P^- are false, and it is the smaller $P^+ \cup P^-$ such that for every $c \in C$ there exists a property in P^+ that does not hold for c or a property in P^- that holds for c.

We further reuse the orderings from the incremental algorithm for the search process used by the constraints solver.

3.3 Graph Algorithm

The REG graph-based algorithm (Krahmer et al., 2003) constructs an initial directed graph G that models the original problem. The nodes in G belong to $\{R\} \cup C$ and the edges represent the properties P. The algorithm recursively constructs a

---

[1] At this level in the generation pipeline, the system operates on abstract semantic representations, the actual words and syntactic forms are left to other components, such as the lexical chooser and the surface generator. In this discussion we use nominal phrases to illustrate the topics, but this is with the understanding that is the output of the full system not the REG algorithm alone.

[2] https://github.com/DrDub/Alusivo

[3] We employed the Choco CSP solver Java library: http://choco-solver.org/.

sub-graph of G, V, starting with node R. At each step it explores the space of successors of the nodes in G that are not in V. The search is guided by a cost function that is calculated each time a node and edge are added to V. The goal of the algorithm is to check whether the properties in V serve to distinguish R from C, meaning that V is distinctive. To verify whether V is distinctive, at each step the algorithm searches for the existence of a sub-graph G_c isomorphic to V, where G_c contains a node $c \in C$; if no such graph exists, then V is distinctive. Finally, the least expensive distinctive graph is returned.

Different cost functions are possible. For our experiments, we use a cost function equal to the number of edges plus the number of vertices in the subgraph and we order the search over edges using the same ordering as the incremental algorithm. This is the particular parameterization of the graph algorithm that we are comparing against the other algorithms.

4 Data

We have chosen Wikipedia as our source of entities, as it represents one of the biggest freely available knowledge base. Started in January 2001 at present it contains over 37 million articles in 284 languages and it continues to grow thanks to the collaborative creation of content by thousands of users around the globe.

Given that the content in Wikipedia pages is stored in a structured way, it is possible to extract and organize it in an ontology-like manner as implemented in the DBpedia community project. This is accomplished by mapping Wikipedia infoboxes from each page to a curated shared ontology that contains 529 classes and around 2,330 different properties. DBpedia contains the knowledge from 111 different language editions of Wikipedia and, for English the knowledge base consists of more than 400 million facts describing 3.7 million things (Lehmann et al., 2015). A noble feature of this resource is that it is freely available to download in the form of *dumps* or it can be consulted using specific tools developed to query it.

These dumps contain the information coded in a language called Resource Description Framework (RDF) (Lassila et al., 1998). The WWW Consortium (W3C) has developed RDF to encode the knowledge present in web pages, so that it is comprehensible and exploitable by agents during any information search. RDF is based on the concept of making statements about (Web) resources using expressions in the subject-predicate-object form. These expressions are known as triples, where the subject denotes the resource being described, the predicate denotes a characteristic of the subject and describes the relation between the subject and the object. A collection of such RDF declarations can be formally represented as a labeled directed multi-graph, naturally appropriate to represent ontologies.

We have chosen to use the dumps of different versions of Wikipedia, namely versions 2014 (09/2014) and 3.6 (01/2011). DBpedia 3.6 ontology encompasses 359 classes and 1,775 properties (800 object properties, 859 datatype properties using standard units, 116 datatype properties using specialized units) and DBpedia 2014 ontology encompasses 685 classes and 2,795 properties (1,079 object properties, 1,600 datatype properties using standard units, 116 datatype properties using specialized units).[4] These versions have been specifically selected: the 2014 version for current up-to-date data and the 3.8 version for comparison with the results by Pacheco et al. (Pacheco et al., 2012).

5 Experimental setup

We follow an approach similar to Pacheco et al. (Pacheco et al., 2012) to extract REG tasks from journalistic text: we extract all people that appear explicitly linked in a given Wikinews article. By using Wikinews, we ensure all the people are disambiguated to their DBpedia URIs by construction (Figure 1).[5] We selected a Wikinews dump as closest to our target DBpedia (20140901). From there, we define all URIs for which DBpedia has a birthDate relation (761,830 entities) as "people" and all entities with a foundDate as an "organization" (19,694 entities). We extract all such people and organizations that appear in the same Wikinews article using the provided inter-wiki SQL links file. For each article, we randomly chose a person as the referent, turning them into a fully defined REG task. This approach produced 4,741 different REG tasks, over 9,660 different people and 3,062 over 8,539

---

[4]Statistics taken from the DBpedia change log available at http://wiki.dbpedia.org/services-resources/datasets/change-log.

[5]These are *potential* REG tasks, but not *actual* REG tasks. We use the news article to extract naturally co-occurring entities.

Algorithm	Execution Errors	Dice	Omission Errors	Inclusion Errors
People				
Incremental	232 (5%)	0.48	1,406 (50%)	145 (5%)
Gardent	0 (0%)	0.58	1,089 (36%)	554 (18%)
Graph	15 (0%)	0.38	1,870 (62%)	20 (0%)
Organizations				
Incremental	1,386 (45%)	0.69	305 (31%)	3 (0%)
Gardent	829 (27%)	0.70	338 (22%)	357 (23%)
Graph	934 (31%)	0.06	1,347 (94%)	2 (0%)

Table 1: Our results, over 3,051 different REG tasks for people and 2,370 for organizations. The error percentages are computed over the total number of executed tasks.

organizations. Each REG task has an average of 4.89 people and 2.79 organizations.

We then created a subset of the relevant tuples for these people (291,039 tuples on DBpedia 2014 and 129,782 on DBpedia 3.6, a 224% increase[6]) and organizations (468,041 tuples on DBpedia 2014 and 216,730 on DBpedia 3.6, a 216% increase) by extracting all tuples were any of the people or organizations were involved, either as subject or object of the statement. Over these subsets were our algorithms executed.

As we are interested in REs occurring after first mentions, we filter properties from the data that unequivocally identify the entity, such as full name or GPS location of its headquarters.

6 Results

We run three representative algorithms that can deal with single entity referents, described in Section 3. As all our algorithms can fail to produce a RE, the first column in our results table (Table 1) contains the number of execution errors. The algorithms can fail either because they have a time-out argument (such as in Graph) or they have a restricted set of heuristics (like IA) that might fail to produce a unique description. In the event of unknown entities (36% of people tasks and 23% of organization tasks contain an entity unknown to DBpedia 3.6), Gardent Algorithm can attempt to produce a RE using negations (using a closed world assumption) while our implementation of the Graph Algorithm will also attempt building a RE if the unknown entity is not the referent. This seldom happens and we report only numbers on

---

[6]In DBpedia 2014, there was an average of 30.12 properties per person while in DBpedia 3.6, there was an average of 17.3

fully defined tasks, which mean the algorithms can be run only on 64% of people tasks and 77% of organization tasks. Using the RE obtained in the old version of DBpedia, we executed on the new version and computed a Dice set similarity coefficient between the two sets. However, Dice has its own problems when it comes to evaluating REG results (van Deemter and Gatt, 2009) and we thus computed two extra metrics: inclusion errors and omission errors. Inclusion errors imply the RE chosen on the old version of DBpedia included extra distractors when applied to the new version of DBpedia. Omission errors imply the RE chosen on the old version of DBpedia failed to include the referent in the new version (this figure includes all execution errors).

The number of inclusion errors is somewhat in line with our expectations from having a more detailed ontological resource: as more data is known about the world, properties that seemed a good fit in a knowledge poor situation all of sudden become too general. For example, trying to distinguish a politician A from two other politicians B, C when we do not have a record that B and C are politicians will lead us to a RE (x *is a politician*) that will overgenerate on a newer, richer ontology.

The number of omission errors was, however, puzzling at first sight and wholesome unacceptable. A certain level of omission errors can be expected (referring to a former prime minister as a prime minister will result in an omission error) but a 3 year span cannot justify 50% omission errors. Further error analysis reveals two key changes in DBpedia that result in this behavior: a re-engineering of its type system (dropping large number of types, such as 'Politician') and dropping language annotations for values (from "22nd"@en to "22nd" –note the dropping of @en). These two changes account for 90% of the omission errors and even a greater percentage of the errors produced by the Graph Algorithm in organizations (the 0.06 Dice in the table).

Now, with further engineering on our behalf (or by choosing a different version of DBpedia where these changes have been already ironed out), we can have an experiment that will shed more light over which REG algorithm is more robust. However, for the sake of our first research question, we find these results quite enlightening: these ontological changes were difficult to spot (the new version was 200% *bigger*, there were little reason to expect many types were *dropped*). Moreover, type information is key for most REG algorithms. We believe this highlights a different point-of-view when designing NLG subcomponents that operate with real data in a changing world.

Given this, our results are too early to fully compare REG algorithms but as a preliminary result, the CSP approach seems to perform consistently at the top. We also found a few interesting examples presented in the appendix.

All our code and data are available online for further analysis.[7]

7   Conclusions

We set ourselves to investigate the robustness of a NLG subcomponent when applied to Web data in RDF format. We were interested in two different phenomena: (1) whether an NLG subcomponent (REG in particular) can be used with outdated ontological data to fulfill its task and (2) which implementation of said subcomponent is better suited to this setting. Our research is driven by the second question but this current work sheds more light on the first one: we found that, off the bat, one quarter of the entities of interest, using three year old data, will be unknown. Handling unknown ontological entities is a problem that has received no attention in NLG as far as we can tell (compare this to dealing with OOV words in NLU, a well defined task and problem). Moreover, we found that in the particular span we have chosen, the typesystem underwent massive re-engineering, which in turn renders the old referring expres-

```
Former [[New Mexico]] {{w|Governor of New
Mexico|governor}} {{w|Gary Johnson}} ended
his campaign for the {{w|Republican Party
(United States)|Republican Party}} (GOP)
presidential nomination to seek the backing
of the {{w|Libertarian Party (United
States)|Libertarian Party}} (LP).
```

Figure 1: Wikinews example, from `http://en.wikinews.org /wiki/U.S. _presidential _candidate _Gary _Johnson _leaves _GOP _to _vie _for _the _LP _nom`, adapted from Pacheco et al. (Pacheco et al., 2012).

sions meaningless for this exercise[8] (and renders their associated resources, such as lexicons, stale). Given these errors, it is still too early to conclude which algorithm from the three REG algorithms we analyzed fares better in this setting, but we found early evidence in favor of the constraint satisfaction algorithm proposed by Gardent (2002). We also believe that there is space for a new REG algorithm design with resiliency in mind that seeks to produce REs that hold better over time.

Our comparison has been done over three specifically parameterized versions of the chosen algorithms. We cannot conclude whether the differences among them are due to differences in the algorithms themselves or in their parameterizations. We believe a follow-up study measuring the impact of different parameterizations in this setting is merited.

Also in future work, we plan to simulate natural perturbations on the data in order to find the conditions on which REG algorithms start to fail (for example, a simulated DBpedia of 25 years in the future).

Acknowledgments

We would like to thank the anonymous reviewers as well as Annie Ying and Victoria Reggiardo.

References

C. Bizer, J. Lehmann, G. Kobilarov, S. Auer, C. Becker, R. Cyganiak, and S. Hellmann. 2009. DBpedia-a crystallization point for the web of data. *Web Semantics: Science, Services and Agents on the World Wide Web*, 7(3):154–165.

B. Bohnet. 2007. is-fbn, is-fbs, is-iac: The adaptation of two classic algorithms for the generation of referring expressions in order to produce expressions like

---

⁷`https://github.com/DrDub/Alusivo` and `https://duboue.net/data`.

⁸Whether or not the RE still hold in the real world is a topic we did not investigate, given the size of our evaluation.

humans do. *MT Summit XI, UCNLG+ MT*, pages 84–86.

Lynne Cahill, John Carroll, Roger Evans, Daniel Paiva, Richard Power, Donia Scott, and Kees van Deemter. 2001. From rags to riches: exploiting the potential of a flexible generation architecture. In *Proceedings of the 39th Annual Meeting on Association for Computational Linguistics*, pages 106–113. Association for Computational Linguistics.

R. Dale and E. Reiter. 1995. Computational interpretations of the gricean maxims in the generation of referring expressions. *Cognitive Science*, 19(2):233–263.

Pablo Duboue and Martín Domínguez. 2016. Using robustness to learn to order semantic properties in referring expression generation. In *Proceedings of Iberamia 2016 (to appear)*.

Pablo Duboue, Martín Domínguez, and Paula Estrella. 2015. Evaluating robustness of referring expression generation algorithms. In *Proceedings of Mexican International Conference on Artificial Intelligence 2015*. IEEE Computer Society.

Johann Eder and Christian Koncilia. 2004. C.: Modelling changes in ontologies. In *In: Proceedings of On The Move - Federated Conferences, OTM 2004, Springer (2004) LNCS 3292*, pages 662–673.

C. Gardent. 2002. Generating minimal definite descriptions. In *Proceedings of the 40th Annual Meeting on Association for Computational Linguistics*, pages 96–103. Association for Computational Linguistics.

Tomi Kauppinen and Eero Hyvnen. 2007. Modeling and reasoning about changes in ontology time series. In *Integrated Series in Information Systems*, pages 319–338. Springer-Verlag.

Emiel Krahmer, Sebastiaan Erk, and Andr Verleg. 2003. Graph-based generation of referring expressions. *Computational Linguistics*, 29:53–72.

Roman Kutlak, Kees van Deemter, and Chris Mellish. 2013. Generation of referring expressions in large domains. *PRE-CogSci, Berlin*.

Jean-Louis Lassez. 1987. Logic programming. In *Proceedings of the Fourth International Conference*.

Ora Lassila, Ralph R. Swick, World Wide, and Web Consortium. 1998. Resource description framework (rdf) model and syntax specification.

Jens Lehmann, Robert Isele, Max Jakob, Anja Jentzsch, Dimitris Kontokostas, Pablo N. Mendes, Sebastian Hellmann, Mohamed Morsey, Patrick van Kleef, Sören Auer, and Christian Bizer. 2015. DBpedia - a large-scale, multilingual knowledge base extracted from wikipedia. *Semantic Web Journal*, 6(2):167–195.

Fabián Pacheco, Pablo Ariel Duboue, and Martín Ariel Domínguez. 2012. On the feasibility of open domain referring expression generation using large scale folksonomies. In *Proceedings of the 2012 Conference of the North American Chapter of the Association for Computational Linguistics: Human Language Technologies*, NAACL HLT '12, pages 641–645, Stroudsburg, PA, USA. Association for Computational Linguistics.

Fabián Pacheco. 2012. Evaluacin en gran escala de algoritmos clsicos parade expresiones referenciales generacin. Master's thesis, Facultad de Matematica Astronomia y Fisica, Universidad Nacional de Cordoba.

Anisa Rula, Luca Panziera, Matteo Palmonari, and Andrea Maurino. 2014. Capturing the currency of dbpedia descriptions and get insight into their validity. In *Proceedings of the 5th International Workshop on Consuming Linked Data (COLD 2014) co-located with the 13th International Semantic Web Conference (ISWC 2014), Riva del Garda, Italy, October 20, 2014*.

Kees van Deemter and Albert Gatt. 2009. Beyond dice: measuring the quality of a referring expression. In *Proceedings of the Workshop on Production of Referring Expressions: Bridging Computational and Psycholinguistic Approaches*.

- Distinguish *Saddam Hussein* from *Paul Volcker, Kofi Annan, Boutros Boutros-Ghali*

  Incr orderInOffice: "President of Iraq"
  Gardent orderInOffice: "President of Iraq"
  Graph activeYearsEndDate: 2006-12-30

  All algorithms perform well.

- Distinguish *Daniel Vettori* from *Kyle Mills*

  Incr country: New Zealand
  Gardent NOT country: New Zealand national cricket team
  ***Graph** description: "New Zealand cricketer"

  Here the accuracy of the information comes into play. Both people are New Zealand cricketers but the information on Mills is poorer than on Vettori. The REs for all algorithms are incorrect but work due to lack of data on Mills. In the new version of DBpedia the description attribute for Mills has been added and now Graph fails. The other two algorithms still work well, even if they should not.

- Distinguish *Park Geun-hye* from *Martin Dempsey*

  Incr type: Office Holder
  Gardent NOT type: Military Person
  ***Graph** birth year: 1952

  This is very curious, both people are born in the same year, but that information was missing in the old version of DBpedia for the distractor.

- Distinguish *Paul McCartney* from *Ringo Starr, John Lennon, George Harrison*

  Incr instrument: Hfner 500/1
  Gardent NOT associated musical artist: Plastic Ono Band
  ***Graph** background: solo singer

  In the old DBpedia, McCartney was the only Beatle marked as a solo singer, while in the new version all of them are. Note how Gardent picks having not played in the Plastic Ono Band as McCartney's most distinguishing feature from the rest.

- Distinguish *Vazgen Sargsyan* from *Karen Demirchyan, Paruyr Hayrikyan, Serzh Sargsyan, Hovik Abrahamyan*

  Incr type: Office Holder, Politician, Prime Minister
  Gardent type: Prime Minister
  ***Graph** death date: 1999-10-27

  Both Sargsyan and Demirchyan died in a tragic shooting at the Armenian parliament. That information was not recorded in the old DBpedia for Demirchyan, leading to the error.

Content Selection through Paraphrase Detection: Capturing different Semantic Realisations of the Same Idea

Elena Lloret
University of Alicante
Alicante, Spain
elloret@dlsi.ua.es

Claire Gardent
CNRS/LORIA
Nancy, France
claire.gardent@loria.fr

1 Introduction

Summarisation can be seen as an instance of Natural Language Generation (NLG), where *"what to say"* corresponds to the identification of relevant information, and *"how to say it"* would be associated to the final creation of the summary. When dealing with data coming from the Semantic Web (e.g., RDF triples), the challenge of how a good summary can be produced arises. For instance, having the RDF properties from an infobox of a Wikipedia page, how could a summary expressed in natural language text be generated? and how could this summary sound as natural as possible (i.e., be an abstractive summary) far from only being a bunch of selected sentences output together (i.e., extractive summary)? This would imply to be able to successfully map the RDF information to a semantic representation of natural language sentences (e.g., predicate-argument (*pred-arg*) structures). Towards the long-term objective of generating abstractive summaries from Semantic Web data, the specific goal of this paper is to propose and validate an approach to map linguistic structures that can encode the same meaning but with different words (e.g., sentence-to-sentence, *pred-arg*-to-*pred-arg*, RDF-to-TEXT) using continuous semantic representation of text. The idea is to decide the level of document representation to work with; convert the text into that representation; and perform a pairwise comparison to decide to what extent two pairs can be mapped or not. For achieving this, different methods were analysed, including traditional Wordnet-based ones, as well as more recent ones based on word embeddings. Our approach was tested and validated in the context of document-abstract sentence mapping to check whether it was appropriate for identifying important information. The results obtained good performance, thus indicating that we can rely on the approach and apply it to further contexts (e.g., mapping RDFs into natural language).

The remainder of this paper is organised as follows: Section 2 outlines related work. Section 3 explains the proposed approach for mapping linguistic units. Section 4 describes our dataset and experiments. Section 5 provides the results and discussion. Finally, Section 6 draws the main conclusions and highlights possible futures directions.

2 Related Work

Abstractive summarisation is one of the most challenging issues to address automatically, since it both requires deep language understanding and generation with a strong semantic component. For tackling this task, approaches usually need to define an internal representation of the text, that can be in the form of SVO triples (Genest and Lapalme, 2011), basic semantic units consisting of *actor-action-receiver* (Li, 2015), or using *pred-arg* structures (Khan et al., 2015). In this latter work, *pred-arg* structures extracted from different related documents are compared, so that common or redundant information can be grouped into clusters. For computing a similarity matrix, Wordnet[1]-based similarity metrics are used, mainly relying on the semantic distance between concepts, given Wordnets' hierarchy.

On the other hand, previous works on linguistic structure mapping can be related to paraphrase identification (Fernando and Stevenson, 2008; Xu et al., 2015), as well as to *pred-arg* alignment (Wolfe et al., 2015; Roth and Frank, 2015). However, these works only use semantic similarity metrics based on WordNet or other semantic resources, such as ConceptNet[2] or FrameNet[3].

---

[1]https://wordnet.princeton.edu/
[2]http://conceptnet5.media.mit.edu/
[3]https://framenet.icsi.berkeley.edu/fndrupal/

Proceedings of the 2nd International Workshop on Natural Language Generation and the Semantic Web (WebNLG), pages 25–28,
Edinburgh, Scotland, September 6th, 2016. ©2016 Association for Computational Linguistics

The use of continuous semantic representation, and in particular the learning or use of Word Embeddings (WE) has been shown to be more appropriate and powerful approach for representing linguistic elements (words, sentences, paragraphs or documents) (Turian et al., 2010; Dai et al., 2015). Given its good performance, they have been recently applied to many natural language generation tasks (Collobert et al., 2011; Kågebäck et al., 2014). The work presented in (Perez-Beltrachini and Gardent, 2016) proposes a method to learn embeddings to lexicalise RDF properties, showing also the potential of using this type of representation for the Semantic Web.

3 Our Mapping Approach

Our approach mainly consists of three stages: i) identification and extraction of text semantic structures; ii) representation of these semantic structures in a continuous vector space; and iii) define and compute the similarity between two representations.

For the first stage, depending on the level defined for the linguistic elements (e.g., a clause, a sentence, a paragraph), a text processing is carried out, using the appropriate tools to obtain the desired structures (e.g., sentence segmentation, semantic role labelling, syntactic parsing, etc.). Then, in the second stage, we represent each structure through its WEs. If the structure consists of more than one element, we will compute the final vector as the composition of the WEs of each of the elements it contains. This is a common strategy that has been previously adopted, in which the addition or product normally lead to the best results (Mitchell and Lapata, 2008; Blacoe and Lapata, 2012; Kågebäck et al., 2014). Finally, the aim of the third stage is to define a similarity metric between the vectors obtained in the second stage.

4 Dataset and Approach Configuration

The English training collection of documents and abstracts from the Single document Summarization task (MSS)[4] of the MultiLing2015 was used as corpus. It consisted of 30 Wikipedia documents from heterogeneous topics (e.g., history of Texas University, fauna of Australia, or Magic Johnson) and their abstracts, which corresponded to the introductory paragraphs of the Wikipedia page. Documents were rather long, having 3,972 words on average (the longest document had 8,348 words and the shortest 2,091), whereas abstracts were 274 words on average (the maximum value was 305 words and the minimum 243), thus resulting in a very low compression ratio[5] - around 7%.

For carrying out the experiments, our approach receives document-abstract pairs as input. These correspond to the source documents, as well as the abstracts associated to those documents. Following the stages defined in Section 3, both were segmented in sentences, and the *pred-arg* structures were automatically identified using SENNA semantic role labeller [6]. Different configurations were tested as far as the WE and the similarity metrics were concerned for the second and third stages. For representing either sentences or *pred-arg* structures, GLoVe pre-trained WE vectors (Pennington et al., 2014) were used, specifically the ones derived from Wikipedia 2014 + Gigaword 5 corpora, containing around 6 billion tokens; and the ones derived from a Common Crawl, with 840 billion tokens. Regarding the similarity metrics, Wordnet-based metrics included the shortest path between synsets, Leacock-Chodorow similarity, Wu-Palmer similarity, Resnik similarity, Jiang-Conrath similarity, and Lin similarity, all of them implemented in NLTK[7]. For the WE settings, the similarity metrics were computed on the basis of the cosine similarity and the Euclidean distance. These latter metrics were applied upon the two composition methods for sentence embedding representations: addition and product, as described in (Blacoe and Lapata, 2012). In the end, a total of 38 distinct configurations were obtained.

5 Evaluation and Discussion

We addressed the validation of the source document-abstract pairs mapping as an extrinsic task using ROUGE (Lin, 2004). ROUGE is a well-known tool employed for summarisation evaluation, which computes the n-gram overlapping between an automatic and a reference summary in terms of n-grams (unigrams - ROUGE 1; bigrams - ROUGE 2, etc.). Our assumption behind this type of evaluation was that considering the

---

[4]http://multiling.iit.demokritos.gr/pages/view/1532/task-mss-single-document-summarization-data-and-information

[5]The compression ratio is the size of the summary with respect to the source document, i.e., the percentage of relevant information to be kept.

[6]http://ronan.collobert.com/senna/

[7]http://www.nltk.org/

	ROUGE-1			ROUGE-2			ROUGE-SU4		
	R	P	F	R	P	F	R	P	F
TEXT baseline	41.63	40.64	41.11	10.11	9.87	9.99	15.67	15.29	15.45
Best TEXT+ WORDNET	42.04	41.58	41.78	11.40	11.25	11.32	16.55	16.34	16.43
Best TEXT+ WE	**50.36**	**47.99**	**49.12**	**17.35**	**16.56**	**16.94**	**22.51**	**21.46**	**21.96**
PRED-ARG baseline	34.64	34.05	34.24	7.19	7.09	7.12	12.25	12.04	12.10
Best PRED-ARG + WORDNET	38.45	38.45	38.39	9.97	9.98	9.96	14.79	14.80	14.77
Best PRED-ARG + WE	**46.88**	**45.17**	**45.97**	**15.18**	**14.53**	**14.84**	**20.02**	**19.23**	**15.60**

Table 1: Results (in percentages) for the extrinsic validation of the mapping.

source document snippets of the top-ranked mapping pairs, and directly building a summary with them (i.e., an extractive summary), good ROUGE results should be obtained if the mapping was good enough.

Table 1 reports the most relevant results obtained. As baselines, we considered the ROUGE direct comparison between the sentences (or *pred-arg* structures) of the source document and the ones in the abstract (TEXT baseline, and PRED-ARG baseline, respectively). We report the results for ROUGE-1, ROUGE-2 and ROUGE-SU4[8]. The results obtained show that representing the semantics of a sentence or *pred-arg* structure using WE leads to the best results, improving those from traditional WordNet-based similarity metrics. The best approach for the WE configuration corresponds to the addition composition method with cosine similarity, and using the pre-trained WE derived from Wikipedia+GigaWord. Compared to the state of the art in summarisation, the results with WE are also encouraging, since previous published results with the same corpus (Alcón and Lloret, 2015) are close to 44% (F-measure for ROUGE-1).

Concerning the comparison between whether using the whole text with respect to only using the *pred-arg* structures, the former gets better results. This is logical since the more text to compare, the higher chances to obtain similar n-grams when evaluating with ROUGE. However, this also limits the capability of abstractive summarisation systems, since we would end up with selecting the sentences as they are, thus restricting the method to purely extractive. Nevertheless, the results obtained by the use of *pred-arg* structures are still reasonably acceptable, and this type of structure would allow to generalise the key content to be selected that should be later rephrased in a proper sentence, producing an abstractive sum-

mary. Next, we provide the top 3 best pair alignments (source document— abstract) of the highest performing configuration using *pred-arg* structure as examples. The value in brackets mean the similarity percentage obtained by our approach.

protected areas — protected areas (100%)
the insects comprising 75% of Australia 's known species of animals —The fauna of Australia consists of a huge variety of strange and unique animals ; some 83% of mammals, 89% of reptiles, 90% of fish and insects (99.94%)
European settlement , direct exploitation of native faun , habitat destruction and the introduction of exotic predators and competitive herbivores led to the extinction of some 27 mammal, 23 bird and 4 frog species. — Hunting, the introduction of non- native species, and land - management practices involving the modification or destruction of habitats led to numerous extinctions (99.93%)

Finally, our intuition behind the results obtained (maximum values of 50%) is that not all the information in the abstract can be mapped with the information of the source document, indicating that a proper abstract may contain extra information that provides from the world knowledge of its author.

6 Conclusion and Future Work

This paper presented an approach to automatically map linguistic structures using continuous semantic representation of sentences. The analysis conducted over a wide set of configuration showed that the use of WEs improves the results compared to traditional WordNet-based metrics, thus being suitable to be employed in data-to-text NLG approaches that need to align content from the Semantic Web to text in natural language. As future work, we plan to evaluate the approach intrinsically and apply it to map non-linguistic in-

---

[8]ROUGE-SU4 accounts for skip-bigrams with maximum gap length of 4.

formation (e.g., RDF) to natural language. We would also like to use the proposed method to create training positive and negative instances to learn classification models for content selection.

Acknowledgments

This research work has been partially funded by the University of Alicante, Generalitat Valenciana, Spanish Government and the European Commission through the projects, "Explotación y tratamiento de la información disponible en Internet para la anotación y generación de textos adaptados al usuario" (GRE13-15) and "DIIM2.0: Desarrollo de técnicas Inteligentes e Interactivas de Minería y generación de información sobre la web 2.0" (PROMETEOII/2014/001), TIN2015-65100-R, TIN2015-65136-C2-2-R, and SAM (FP7-611312), respectively.

References

Óscar Alcón and Elena Lloret. 2015. Estudio de la influencia de incorporar conocimiento léxico-semántico a la técnica de análisis de componentes principales para la generación de resúmenes multilingües. *Linguamatica*, 7(1):53–63, July.

William Blacoe and Mirella Lapata. 2012. A comparison of vector-based representations for semantic composition. In *Proceedings of the 2012 Joint Conference on Empirical Methods in Natural Language Processing and Computational Natural Language Learning*, pages 546–556, Jeju Island, Korea, July. Association for Computational Linguistics.

Ronan Collobert, Jason Weston, Léon Bottou, Michael Karlen, Koray Kavukcuoglu, and Pavel Kuksa. 2011. Natural language processing (almost) from scratch. *J. Mach. Learn. Res.*, 12:2493–2537, November.

Andrew M. Dai, Christopher Olah, and Quoc V. Le. 2015. Document embedding with paragraph vectors. *CoRR*, abs/1507.07998.

Samuel Fernando and Mark Stevenson. 2008. A semantic similarity approach to paraphrase detection. *Computational Linguistics UK (CLUK 2008) 11th Annual Research Colloqium*.

Pierre-Etienne Genest and Guy Lapalme. 2011. Framework for abstractive summarization using text-to-text generation. In *Proceedings of the Workshop on Monolingual Text-To-Text Generation*, MTTG '11, pages 64–73, Stroudsburg, PA, USA. Association for Computational Linguistics.

Atif Khan, Naomie Salim, and Yogan Jaya Kumar. 2015. A framework for multi-document abstractive summarization based on semantic role labelling. *Appl. Soft Comput.*, 30(C):737–747, May.

Mikael Kågebäck, Olof Mogren, Nina Tahmasebi, and Devdatt Dubhashi. 2014. Extractive summarization using continuous vector space models. In *Proceedings of the 2nd Workshop on Continuous Vector Space Models and their Compositionality (CVSC)*, pages 31–39, Gothenburg, Sweden, April. Association for Computational Linguistics.

Wei Li. 2015. Abstractive multi-document summarization with semantic information extraction. In *Proceedings of the 2015 Conference on Empirical Methods in Natural Language Processing*, pages 1908–1913, Lisbon, Portugal, September. Association for Computational Linguistics.

Chin-Yew Lin. 2004. Rouge: A package for automatic evaluation of summaries. In Stan Szpakowicz Marie-Francine Moens, editor, *Text Summarization Branches Out: Proceedings of the ACL-04 Workshop*, pages 74–81, Barcelona, Spain, July. Association for Computational Linguistics.

Jeff Mitchell and Mirella Lapata. 2008. Vector-based models of semantic composition. In *Proceedings of ACL-08: HLT*, pages 236–244, Columbus, Ohio, June. Association for Computational Linguistics.

Jeffrey Pennington, Richard Socher, and Christopher D. Manning. 2014. Glove: Global vectors for word representation. In *Empirical Methods in Natural Language Processing (EMNLP)*, pages 1532–1543.

Laura Perez-Beltrachini and Claire Gardent. 2016. Learning Embeddings to lexicalise RDF Properties. In **SEM 2016: The Fifth Joint Conference on Lexical and Computational Semantics*, Berlin, Germany.

Michael Roth and Anette Frank. 2015. Inducing Implicit Arguments from Comparable Texts: A Framework and its Applications. *Computational Linguistics*, 41:625–664.

Joseph Turian, Lev Ratinov, and Yoshua Bengio. 2010. Word representations: A simple and general method for semi-supervised learning. In *Proceedings of the 48th Annual Meeting of the Association for Computational Linguistics*, ACL '10, pages 384–394, Stroudsburg, PA, USA. Association for Computational Linguistics.

Travis Wolfe, Mark Dredze, and Benjamin Van Durme. 2015. Predicate argument alignment using a global coherence model. In *Proceedings of the 2015 Conference of the North American Chapter of the Association for Computational Linguistics: Human Language Technologies*, pages 11–20, Denver, Colorado, May–June. Association for Computational Linguistics.

Wei Xu, Chris Callison-Burch, and Bill Dolan. 2015. Semeval-2015 task 1: Paraphrase and semantic similarity in twitter (pit). In *Proceedings of the 9th International Workshop on Semantic Evaluation (SemEval 2015)*, pages 1–11, Denver, Colorado, June. Association for Computational Linguistics.

Aligning Texts and Knowledge Bases with Semantic Sentence Simplification

Yassine Mrabet[1,3], Pavlos Vougiouklis[2], Halil Kilicoglu[1],
Claire Gardent[3], Dina Demner-Fushman[1], Jonathon Hare[2], and Elena Simperl[2]

[1]Lister Hill National Center for Biomedical Communications
National Library of Medicine, USA
{mrabety,kilicogluh,ddemner}@mail.nih.gov

[2]Web and Internet Science Research Group
University of Southampton, UK
{pv1e13,jsh2,es}@ecs.soton.ac.uk

[3]CNRS/LORIA, France
claire.gardent@loria.fr

Abstract

Finding the natural language equivalent of structured data is both a challenging and promising task. In particular, an efficient alignment of knowledge bases with texts would benefit many applications, including natural language generation, information retrieval and text simplification. In this paper, we present an approach to build a dataset of triples aligned with equivalent sentences written in natural language. Our approach consists of three main steps. First, target sentences are annotated automatically with knowledge base (KB) concepts and instances. The triples linking these elements in the KB are extracted as candidate facts to be aligned with the annotated sentence. Second, we use textual mentions referring to the subject and object of these facts to semantically simplify the target sentence via crowdsourcing. Third, the sentences provided by different contributors are post-processed to keep only the most relevant simplifications for the alignment with KB facts. We present different filtering methods, and share the constructed datasets in the public domain. These datasets contain 1,050 sentences aligned with 1,885 triples. They can be used to train natural language generators as well as semantic or contextual text simplifiers.

1 Introduction

A large part of the information on the Web is contained in databases and is not suited to be directly accessed by human users. A proper exploitation of these data requires relevant visualization techniques which may range from simple tabular presentation with meaningful queries, to graph generation and textual description. This last type of visualization is particularly interesting as it produces an additional raw resource that can be read by both computational agents (e.g. search engines) and human users. From this perspective, the ability to generate high quality text from knowledge and data bases could be a game changer.

In the Natural language Processing community, this task is known as Natural Language Generation (NLG). Efficient NLG solutions would allow displaying the content of knowledge and data bases to lay users; generating explanations, descriptions and summaries from ontologies and linked open data[1]; or guiding the user in formulating knowledge-base queries.

However, one strong and persistent limitation to the development of adequate NLG solutions for the semantic web is the lack of appropriate datasets on which to train NLG models. The difficulty is that the semantic data available in knowledge and data bases need to be aligned with the corresponding text. Unfortunately, this alignment task is far from straightforward. In fact, both human beings and machines perform poorly on it.

---

[1]http://www.linkeddata.org

Proceedings of the 2nd International Workshop on Natural Language Generation and the Semantic Web (WebNLG), pages 29–36,
Edinburgh, Scotland, September 6th, 2016. ©2016 Association for Computational Linguistics

Nonetheless, there has been much work on data-to-text generation and different strategies have been used to create the data-to-text corpora that are required for learning and testing. Two main such strategies can be identified. One strategy consists in creating a small, domain-specific corpus where data and text are manually aligned by a small group of experts (often the researchers who work on developing the NLG system). Typically, such corpora are domain specific and of relatively small size while their linguistic variability is often restricted.

A second strategy consists in automatically building a large data-to-text corpus in which the alignment between data and text is much looser. For instance, Lebret et al. (2016) extracted a corpus consisting of 728,321 biography articles from English Wikipedia and created a data-to-text corpus by simply associating the infobox of each article with its introduction section. The resulting dataset has a vocabulary of 403k words but there is no guarantee that the text actually matches the content of the infobox.

In this paper, we explore a middle-ground approach and introduce a new methodology for semi-automatically building large, high quality data-to-text corpora. More precisely, our approach relies on a semantic sentence simplification method which allows transforming existing corpora into sentences aligned with KB facts. Contrary to manual methods, our approach does not rely on having a small group of experts to identify alignments between text and data. Instead, this task is performed (i) by multiple, independent contributors through a crowdsourcing platform, and (ii) by an automatic scoring of the quality of the contributions, which enables faster and more reliable data creation process. Our approach also departs from the fully automatic approaches (e.g., (Lebret et al., 2016)) in that it ensures a systematic alignment between text and data.

In the following section we present work related to corpus generation for NLG. In section 3 we describe our approach. Section 4 presents the experiments, evaluations, and the statistics on the initial corpora and the generated (aligned) datasets.

2 Related Work

Many studies tackled the construction of datasets for natural language generation. Several available datasets were created by researchers and developers working on NLG systems. Chen and Mooney (2008) created a dataset of text and data describing the Robocup game. To collect the data, they used the Robocup simulator (www.robocup.org) and derived symbolic representations of game events from the simulator traces using a rule-based system. The extracted events are represented as atomic formulas in predicate logic with timestamps. For the natural language portion of the data, they had humans comment games while watching them on the simulator. They manually aligned logical formulas to their corresponding sentences. The resulting data-to-text corpus contains 1,919 scenarios where each scenario consists of a single sentence representing a fragment of a commentary on the game, paired with a set of logical formulas.

The SumTime-Meteo corpus was created by the SumTime project (Sripada et al., 2002). The corpus was collected from the commercial output of five different human forecasters, and each instance in the corpus consists of three numerical data files produced by three different weather simulators, and the weather forecast file written by the forecaster. To train a sentence generator, (Belz, 2008) created a version of the SumTime-Meteo corpus which is restricted to wind data. The resulting corpus consists of 2,123 instances for a total of 22,985 words and was used by other researchers working on NLG and semantic parsing (Angeli et al., 2012).

Other data-to-text corpora were proposed for training and testing generation systems, including WeatherGov (Liang et al., 2009), the ATIS dataset, the Restaurant Corpus (Wen et al., 2015) and the BAGEL dataset (Mairesse et al., 2010). WeatherGov consists of 29,528 weather scenarios for 3,753 major US cities. In the air travel domain, the ATIS dataset (Dahl et al., 1994) consists of 5,426 scenarios. These are transcriptions of spontaneous utterances of users interacting with a hypothetical online flight-booking system. The RESTAURANTS corpus contains utterances that a spoken dialogue system might produce in an interaction with a human user together with the corresponding dialog act. Similarly, the BAGEL dataset is concerned with restaurant information in a dialog setting.

In all these approaches, datasets are created using heuristics often involving extensive manual labour and/or programming. The data is mostly created artificially from sensor or web data rather than extracted from some existing knowledge base. As the data are often domain specific, the vocabulary size and the linguistic variability of the target text are often restricted.

Other approaches tackled the benchmarking of NLG systems and provided the constructed dataset as a publicly available resource. For instance, a Surface Realisation shared task was organised in 2011 to compare and evaluate sentence generators (Belz et al., 2011). The dataset prepared by the organisers was derived from the PennTreebank and associates sentences with both a shallow representation (dependency trees) and a deep representation where edges are labelled with semantic roles (e.g., agent, patient) and the structure is a graph rather than a tree. While the data-to-text corpus that was made available from this shared task was very large, the representation associated with each sentence is a linguistic representation and is not related to a data schema.

The KBGen shared task (Banik et al., 2013) followed a different approach and focused on generating sentences from knowledge bases. For this task, knowledge base fragments were extracted semi-automatically from an existing biology knowledge base (namely, BioKB101 (Chaudhri et al., 2013)) and expert biologists were asked to associate each KB fragments with a sentence verbalising their meaning. The resulting dataset was small (207 data-text instances for training, 70 for testing) and the creation process relied heavily on domain experts, thereby limiting its portability.

In sum, there exists so far no standard methodology for rapidly creating data-to-text corpora that are both sufficiently large to support the training and testing of NLG systems and sufficiently precise to support the development of natural language generation approaches that can map KB data to sentences. The procedures designed by individual researchers to test their own proposals yield data in non-standard formats (e.g., tabular information, dialog acts, infoboxes) and are often limited in size. Data used in shared tasks either fail to associate sentences with knowledge base data (SR shared task) or require extensive manual work and expert validation.

3 Methods

Our approach tackles the conversion of existing textual corpora into a dataset of sentences aligned with <subject, predicate, object> triples collected from existing KBs. It is independent from the selected corpus, domain, or KB.

In the first step, we annotate automatically the target textual corpus by linking textual mentions to knowledge base concepts and instances (KB entities for short). In the second step, we collect triples from the knowledge bases that link the entities mentioned in a given sentence. In the third step, we keep only the mentions that refer to the subject and object of the same triple and perform semantic simplification with a crowdsourcing task. Finally we apply several post-processing algorithms, including clustering and scoring to keep the most relevant semantic simplifications of each sentence as a natural language expression of the set of collected triples.

The alignment that we aim to achieve is not binary, as an output of our approach, one sentence could be aligned with N triples ($N \geq 1$). This property is particularly interesting for NLG as it allows training generation systems on expressing sets of triples in the same sentence; enabling the production of more fluent texts.

3.1 Corpus Annotation and Initial Sentence Selection

In the following we present our methods to obtain automatic initial annotations of the target corpora and to select the sentences that will be used in the final aligned dataset.

3.1.1 Corpus Annotation

In order to have varied empirical observations, we use two different methods for initial corpus annotation. In the **first annotation method** we do not check if the candidate triples are actually expressed in the sentence, only their subjects and objects. This method is particularly suitable to discover new linguistic expressions of triple predicates, and can provide actual expressions of the triple by accumulating observations from different sentences.

To implement this method we use KODA (Mrabet et al., 2015) to link textual mentions to KB entities. KODA is an unsupervised entity linking tool that relies only on the KB contents to detect and disambiguate textual mentions. More precisely, it detects candidate textual mentions with a TF-IDF search on the labels of KB entities, and disambiguates them by maximizing the coherence between the candidate KB entities retrieved for each mention using KB relations.

In the second step we query the KB (e.g., SPARQL endpoint of DBpedia) to obtain the predicates that link the KB entities mentioned in the sentence and keep them as candidate facts. For instance, the 8 highlighted terms in figure 1 were linked to DBpedia entities, but only 4 terms mention KB entities that are linked in DBpedia triples.

This first method is scalable w.r.t. the domain of interest as it can be ported to other KBs with the same implementation.

In the **second annotation method**, we perform the automatic annotation by checking that the triples are actually expressed in the sentence. We use SemRep (Rindflesch and Fiszman, 2003), a biomedical relation extraction system. SemRep extracts binary relations from unstructured texts. The subject and object of these relations are concepts from the UMLS Metathesaurus (Lindberg et al., 1993) and the predicate is a relation type from an expanded version of the UMLS Semantic Network (e.g., *treats, diagnoses, stimulates, inhibits*). SemRep uses MetaMap (Aronson and Lang, 2010) to link noun phrases to UMLS Metathesaurus concepts. For example, the 4 highlighted terms in figure 2 were linked to UMLS concepts and all terms mention either the subject or the object of a relation extracted with SemRep.

In both methods, we keep only the annotations that refer to subjects and objects of candidate facts.

3.1.2 Initial Sentence Selection.

Due to the unsupervised aspect of automatic annotation and the incompleteness of the KBs, some sentences are expected to be annotated more heavily than others, and some sentences are expected to have more triples associated with them than others. In practice, different targets of annotation (e.g. specific semantic categories) could also lead to similar discrepancies.

In order to train automatic sentence simplifiers with our datasets, we have to consider different levels of coverage that can correspond to different annotation tools and dissimilar annotation goals. Accordingly, once the initial corpus is annotated, we select three sets of sentences: (1) a first set of sentences that are *heavily annotated* w.r.t. the number of triples (e.g. between 5 and 10 tokens per triple), (2) a second set with average annotation coverage (e.g. between 10 and 20 tokens per triple), and (3) a third set of weakly annotated sentence (e.g. above 20 tokens per triple).

3.2 Semantic Sentence Simplification (S3)

In order to obtain the final dataset of KB facts aligned with natural language sentences from the initial automatically annotated corpus, we define the task of Semantic Sentence Simplification (S3) and introduce the crowdsourcing process used to perform it.

Definition. Given a sentence S, a set of textual mentions $M(S)$ linked to a set of KB instances and concepts $E(S)$ and a set of triples $T(S) = \{t_i(e_{i_1}, p_i, e_{i_2}), s.t. e_1 \in E(S), e_2 \in E(S)$, the semantic simplification task consists of *shortening the sentence S* as much as possible according to the following rules:

- Keep the textual mentions referring to the subject and object of candidate facts.

- Keep the relations expressed between these textual mentions in the sentence.

- Keep the order of the words from the original sentence as much as possible.

- Ensure that the simplified sentence is grammatical and meaningful.

- Avoid using external words to the extent possible.

Crowdsourcing. We asked contributors to provide simplifications for each sentence through a crowdsourcing platform. We highlighted the textual mentions referring to subjects and objects of candidate facts in these sentences. The contributors are then asked to follow the S3 requirements to shorten the sentences. The quality requirement that was set during the experiment is that each contributor should dedicate at least 15 seconds for each set of 3 sentences.

After several preliminary experiments, we opted for a crowdsourcing process without quiz questions to attract more participants; and we monitored closely the process to filter out irrelevant contributors such as spammers (e.g. people typing in random letters), foreign-language speakers who misunderstood the task and tried to provide translations of the original sentence, and contributors who simply copied the original sentence. By flagging such contributors we also optimized significantly the monitoring for the second corpus.

Mention	DBpedia Entity
Sacco	dbr:Albert_Sacco
payload specialist	dbr:Payload_Specialist
STS-73	dbr:STS-73
October 20	dbr:October_20
1995	dbr:1995
Kennedy Space Center	dbr:Kennedy_Space_Center
November 5	dbr:November_5

Triples		
dbr:Albert_Sacco	dbo:mission	dbr:STS-73
dbr:STS-73	dbp:landingSite	dbr:Kennedy_Space_Center
dbr:STS-73	dbp:launchSite	dbr:Kennedy_Space_Center

Figure 1: Example sentence annotated with DBpedia entities and its candidate triples.

Mention	UMLS Entity
amantadine	C0002403
antiviral agent	C0003451
Parkinson's disease	C0030567
levodopa-induced dyskinesias	C1970038

Triples		
Amantadine	*isa*	Antiviral Agents
Amantadine	*treats*	Parkinson Disease
Amantadine	*treats*	Levodopa-induced dyskinesias

Figure 2: Example sentence annotated with UMLS concepts and triples.

3.3 Selecting the best simplification

In order to select the most relevant simplification for a given sentence from the set of N simplifications proposed by contributors, we test two baseline methods and two advanced scoring methods.

3.3.1 Baselines.

The *first baseline method* is simply the selection of the simplification that has more votes. We will refer to it as $Vote$ in the remainder of the paper. The *second baseline method*, called $Clustering$, is based on the K-Means clustering algorithm. It uses the Euclidean distance measured between word vectors to cluster the set of N simplifications of a given sentence into K clusters. The cluster with the highest cumulative number of votes is selected as the most significant cluster, and the shortest sentence in that cluster is selected as the candidate simplification.

3.3.2 Scoring Methods

Our first selection method scores a simplification according to the original sentence and to the simplification goals expressed in section 3.3. We define four elementary measures to compute a semantic score: *lexical integrity, semantic preservation, conformity* and *relative shortening*. Given an initial sentence s_o and a simplification s_i proposed for s_o, these measures are defined as follows.

Conformity (cnf). The conformity score represents how much the simplification s_i conforms to the rules of the S3 task. It combines lexical integrity and semantic preservation:

$$cnf(s_i, s_o) = \zeta(s_i, s_o) \times \iota(s_i, s_o) \quad (1)$$

Lexical integrity (ι). $\iota(s_i, s_o)$ is the proportion of words in s_i that are in s_o. ι values are in the [0,1] range. The value is lower than 1 if new external words are used.

Semantic Preservation (ζ). Semantic preservation indicates how much of the textual mentions that are linked to KB entities and KB triples are present in the simplification. More precisely, $\zeta(s_i, s_o)$ is the ratio of annotations from s_o that are present in s_i. ζ values are in the [0,1] range.

Relative Shortening (η). Simplifications that are too short might miss important relations or entities, whereas simplifications that are too long might be too close (or equal) to the original sentence. We represent both aspects through a Gaussian and make use of the "wisdom of the crowd" by setting the maximum value at the average length of the simplifications proposed by the contributors. In order to have a moderate decrease around the average, we set both the maximum value and the standard deviation to 1. Length is measured in terms of tokens.

$$\eta(s_i, s_o) = exp(-\frac{(length(s_i) - length_{avg})^2}{2})$$
(2)

Semantic score (ψ). We compute the semantic score for a simplification s_i of s_o by combining the above elements. This combination, expressed in equation 3, is based on the following intuitions: (1) between two simplifications of the same sentence, the difference in conformity should have more impact than the difference in shortening, (2) for the same conformity value, simplifications that are farther from the original sentence are preferred, and (3) simplifications that have a more common shortening extent should be better ranked.

$$\psi(s_i, s_o) = \eta(s_i, s_o) \times exp(cnf(s_i, s_o) \times euclidean(s_i, s_o))$$
(3)

The Euclidean function is the Euclidean distance between the original sentence and the simplification in terms of tokens. Our *second scoring method* relied first on the clustering of the contributors' sentences. As the baseline it identifies the cluster with more votes as most significant. However, the representative sentence is selected according to the semantic score ψ, instead of simply taking the shortest sentence of the cluster. We denote this in-cluster scoring method ξ.

4 Experiments and Results

In the first experiments, we build two datasets of natural language sentences aligned with KB facts.
Corpora and knowledge bases. Our *first dataset* is built by aligning all astronaut pages on Wikipedia[2] (Wiki) with triples from DBpedia[3]. The main motivation behind the choice of this corpus is to have both general and specific relations. We used KODA as described in section 3.1.1 to obtain initial annotations.

Our *second dataset* is built by aligning the medical encyclopedia part of Medline Plus[4] (MLP) with triples extracted with SemRep. The motivation behind the selection of this corpus is twofold: a) to experiment with a domain-specific corpus, and b) to test the simplification when the triples are extracted from the text itself. Table 1 presents raw statistics on each corpus.

	Wiki	MLP
Documents	668	4,360
Sentences	22,820	16,575
Tokens	478,214	421,272
Token per Sentence	20.95	25.41
Triples	15,641	30,342
Triples per Sentence	0.68	1.83
Mentions	64,621	145,308
Arguments	13,751	47,742

Table 1: Basic Statistics on Initial Corpora

Crowdsourcing. We used CrowdFlower[5] as a crowdsourcing platform. We submitted 600 annotated sentences for the Wiki corpus and 450 sentences for the MLP corpus.
Selection of relevant simplifications. We implemented several methods to select the best simplification among the 15 contributions for each sentence (cf. section 3.3). To evaluate these methods we randomly selected 90 initial sentences from each dataset, then extracted the best simplification according to each of the 4 scoring metrics. The authors then rated each simplification from 1 to 5, with 1 indicating a very bad simplification, and 5 indicating an excellent simplification. One of the authors prepared the evaluation tables, anonymized the method names and did not participate in the evaluation. The remaining 6 authors shared the 180 sentences and performed the ratings. Table 2 presents the final average rating for each selection method.

	Baselines		Scoring	
	Vote	Clustering	ξ	ψ
Wiki	**3.62**	3.06	3.51	3.22
MLP	3.51	2.87	**3.61**	3.30
Overall	**3.56**	2.97	**3.56**	3.26

Table 2: Evaluation of S3 Selection Methods (average rating)

Final statistics on aligned datasets. After evalu-

---

[2]https://en.wikipedia.org/wiki/List_of_astronauts_by_name
[3]http://dbpedia.org
[4]https://www.nlm.nih.gov/medlineplus/
[5]http://www.crowdflower.com

	Wiki	**MLP**
Sentences	600	450
Triples	1,119	766
Predicates	146	30
Tokens	13,641	11,167
	(after S3: **9,011**)	(after S3: **6,854**)

Table 3: Statistics on the Aligned Dataset

ating the selection methods we selected the most relevant simplification for each sentence in the dataset according to ξ (i.e., in-cluster scoring), and generated the final datasets that link the best simplification to the facts associated with its original sentence. Table 3 presents the final statistics on the aligned datasets. Both datasets are made available online[6].

Table 4 presents the 10 first predicate names and their distribution for each dataset.

Wiki		**MLP**	
Predicate	%	Predicate	%
rdf:type	15.6	location of	24.93
dbo:type	10.18	is a	20.75
dbo:mission	9.11	process of	14.09
dbo:crewMembers	6.34	treats	7.04
dbo:birthPlace	5.45	causes	6.78
dbo:occupation	4.64	part of	5.87
dbo:nationality	3.30	administred to	3.13
dbo:rank	3.03	coexists with	2.61
dbp:crew2Up	2.94	affects	2.08
dbo:country	1.96	uses	1.43

Table 4: Top 10 predicates

5 Discussion

Automatic Annotation. From our observations on both datasets, we came to the conclusion that uncertainty is required to some extent in the selection of candidate triples. This is due to the fact that relations extracted from the text itself will follow the patterns that were used to find them (e.g., regular expressions, or classifier models) and that will not allow finding enough variation to enrich NLG systems. From this perspective, the best option would be to rank candidate triples according to their probability of occurrence in the sentence

[6] https://github.com/pvougiou/
KB-Text-Alignment

and filter out the triples with very low probability. This ranking and filtering are planned for the final version of our open-domain corpus.

Initial sentence selection. The second goal of our datasets is to be able to train automatic semantic simplifiers that would reduce the need for manual simplification in the long term. Therefore, our first method took into account different levels of annotation coverage in order to cope with different performance/coverage of annotation tools and dissimilar goals in terms of the semantic categories of the mentions. However, for NLG, it is also important to have a balanced number of samples for each unique predicate. The first extension of our datasets will provide a better balance of examples for each predicate while keeping the balance in terms of annotation coverage to the extent possible.

Crowdsourcing. Our crowdsourcing experiment showed that it is possible to obtain relevant semantic simplifications with no specific expertise. This is supported by the fact that the $Vote$ baseline in the selection of the final simplification obtained the same best performance as our scoring method that relies on the semantics of the S3 process. Overall, the experiment cost was only $180 for 15,750 simplifications collected for 1,050 sentences. Our results also show that collecting only 10 simplifications for each sentence (instead of 15 in our experiments) would be more than adequate, which reduces the costs even further. The two jobs created for each dataset were generally well-rated by the contributors (cf. Table 5). The MLP corpus was clearly more accessible than the Wiki corpus with an ease of job estimated at 4.4 vs 3.8 (on a 5 scale). Interestingly, the identical instructions were also rated differently according to the dataset (4.2 vs. 3.8). The Wiki corpus was harder to process, due to the high heterogeneity of the relations and entity categories. There are also fewer arguments per sentence in the Wiki corpus: 0.68 triple per sentence vs. 1.83, for a close average length of 20.95 tokens per sentence vs. 25.41 (cf. Table 1).

	Wiki	MLP
Number of participants	48	41
Clarity of Instructions	3.8	4.2
Ease of Job	3.8	4.4
Overall Rating of Job	3.9	4.4

Table 5: Number of participants and contributors' ratings (on a 1 to 5 scale)

6 Conclusions

We presented a novel approach to build a corpus of natural language sentences aligned with knowledge base facts, and shared the first constructed datasets in the public domain. We introduced the task of semantic sentence simplification that retains only the natural language elements that correspond minimally to KB facts. While our simplification method relied on crowdsourcing, our midterm goal is to collect enough data to train automatic simplifiers that would perform the same task efficiently. Besides the simplification aspect and the portability of the method, the shared datasets are also a valuable resource for natural language generation systems. Future work includes the expansion of these datasets and the improvement of sentence selection using grammatical-quality factors.

Acknowledgments

This work was supported by the intramural research program at the U.S. National Library of Medicine, National Institutes of Health.

References

Gabor Angeli, Christopher D Manning, and Daniel Jurafsky. 2012. Parsing time: Learning to interpret time expressions. In *Proceedings of the 2012 Conference of the North American Chapter of the ACL: Human Language Technologies*, pages 446–455.

Alan R Aronson and François-Michel Lang. 2010. An overview of metamap: historical perspective and recent advances. *JAMIA*, 17(3):229–236.

Eva Banik, Claire Gardent, and Eric Kow. 2013. The kbgen challenge. In *the 14th European Workshop on Natural Language Generation (ENLG)*, pages 94–97.

Anja Belz, Michael White, Dominic Espinosa, Eric Kow, Deirdre Hogan, and Amanda Stent. 2011. The first surface realisation shared task: Overview and evaluation results. In *13th European workshop on natural language generation*, pages 217–226.

Anja Belz. 2008. Automatic generation of weather forecast texts using comprehensive probabilistic generation-space models. *Nat. Language Engineering*, 14(04):431–455.

Vinay K Chaudhri, Michael A Wessel, and Stijn Heymans. 2013. Kb bio 101: A challenge for tptp first-order reasoners. In *CADE-24 Workshop on Knowledge Intensive Automated Reasoning*.

David L Chen and Raymond J Mooney. 2008. Learning to sportscast: a test of grounded language acquisition. In *Proceedings of the 25th ICML conference*, pages 128–135. ACM.

Deborah A Dahl, Madeleine Bates, Michael Brown, William Fisher, Kate Hunicke-Smith, David Pallett, Christine Pao, Alexander Rudnicky, and Elizabeth Shriberg. 1994. Expanding the scope of the atis task: The atis-3 corpus. In *Proceedings of the workshop on Human Language Technology*, pages 43–48. Association for Computational Linguistics.

R. Lebret, D. Grangier, and M. Auli. 2016. Generating Text from Structured Data with Application to the Biography Domain. *ArXiv e-prints*, March.

Percy Liang, Michael I Jordan, and Dan Klein. 2009. Learning semantic correspondences with less supervision. In *Proceedings of the Joint Conference of the 47th Annual Meeting of the ACL and the 4th International Joint Conference on Natural Language Processing of the AFNLP: Volume 1-Volume 1*, pages 91–99.

Donald A Lindberg, Betsy L Humphreys, and Alexa T McCray. 1993. The unified medical language system. *Methods of information in medicine*, 32(4):281–291.

François Mairesse, Milica Gašić, Filip Jurčíček, Simon Keizer, Blaise Thomson, Kai Yu, and Steve Young. 2010. Phrase-based statistical language generation using graphical models and active learning. In *Proceedings of the 48th Annual Meeting of the ACL*, pages 1552–1561. Association for Computational Linguistics.

Yassine Mrabet, Claire Gardent, Muriel Foulonneau, Elena Simperl, and Eric Ras. 2015. Towards knowledge-driven annotation. In *Proceedings of the Twenty-Ninth AAAI Conference on Artificial Intelligence, January 25-30, 2015, Austin, Texas, USA.*, pages 2425–2431.

Thomas C Rindflesch and Marcelo Fiszman. 2003. The interaction of domain knowledge and linguistic structure in natural language processing: interpreting hypernymic propositions in biomedical text. *Journal of biomedical informatics*, 36(6):462–477.

Somayajulu Sripada, Ehud Reiter, Jim Hunter, and Jin Yu. 2002. Sumtime-meteo: Parallel corpus of naturally occurring forecast texts and weather data. *Computing Science Department, University of Aberdeen, Aberdeen, Scotland, Tech. Rep. AUCS/TR0201*.

Tsung-Hsien Wen, Milica Gasic, Nikola Mrksic, Pei-Hao Su, David Vandyke, and Steve Young. 2015. Semantically conditioned lstm-based natural language generation for spoken dialogue systems. *arXiv preprint arXiv:1508.01745*.

Building a System for Stock News Generation in Russian

Liubov Nesterenko

National Research University Higher School of Economics, Moscow

`lyu.klimenchenko@gmail.com`

Abstract

In this paper we present an implementation of an NLG system that serves for stock news generation. The system has two modules: analysis module and NLG module. The first one is intended for processing the data on stock index changes, the second one for the news texts generation using the template-based NLG approach. The evaluation shown that both modules give relatively accurate results and the system can be used as a newsbot for stock news generation.

1 Introduction

The subject of this paper is related to the natural language generation of the stock news.

The stock quotes change considerably during the day, which means that financial media should react quickly to each remarkable change and announce the news very often and very fast. That is why it becomes necessary to make a system that receives the information about latest changes and generates short news on the base of it. In 1983 there was an attempt made by K. Kukich for financial news generation in English (Kukich, 1983). In our paper we present an NLG system for stock news generation in Russian created from scratch, it generates the news having as input the daily data on stock indexes changes.

Our goal is to describe the process of the system implementation and to discuss the problems we had to deal with. Here are the tasks we used to solve as we were working on the system development: choosing methods for index changes analysis, examining the features of financial news texts, collecting financial lexicon, choosing an NLG approach, writing a Python program and evaluating the results. The NLG component uses template-based approach. One of the reasons for that was the lack of an appropriate target corpus of stock news that could make statistical approach, like in (Sutskever et al., 2011), possible. Sometimes the template-based approach is being underestimated but some researches consider that it can be as good as the standard approach (Van Deemter et al., 2005). It could be even combined with some statistical approach, as it was done in (Howald et al., 2013). Moreover, the stock news texts have very clear and simple structure and content, that is why the template-based approach works here quite well.

2 Preliminary work

Our first step was to make some research on index changes and index behavior in general. After that we consulted with the experts on stock news and defined the types of the news that the program should generate. We decided that there are two types of news needed: the morning news and the evening news and that they should be about the changes of two main Russian indexes: MOEX (Moscow Exchange) and RTSI (Russian Trading System Index). Then we explored some financial media resources in order to understand what stock news are like and what features they have. The majority of the stock news on Russian financial media resources appeared to be whether too short (one sentence) or too long (contain lots of information regarding predictions of index future behavior and discussions). That induced us to create our own text layouts for rather short but informative news.

The content and the structure of the news texts are as follows:

Morning News

1. Trades beginning: indexes performance during the first minutes after trades started (general tendency)

2. MOEX index behaviour.

Proceedings of the 2nd International Workshop on Natural Language Generation and the Semantic Web (WebNLG), pages 37–40,
Edinburgh, Scotland, September 6th, 2016. ©2016 Association for Computational Linguistics

3. RTSI index behaviour.

4. The characteristic of the last trading day (generally and particular).

5. MOEX index behaviour yesterday.

6. RTSI index behaviour yesterday.

7. The trades value for the previous trading day.

Evening news

1. General tendency during the day.

2. MOEX index behaviour.

3. RTSI index behaviour.

4. MOEX final change.

5. RTSI final change.

6. The trades value for the day.

These text structures serve as layouts for the news. For each position one should create the suitable templates that will build up the text.

3 Methodology

The system has two components: the analysis module and the NLG module. The first one gets the daily data on indexes as input and determines the index changes using the algorithm we developed for that purpose. As output it gives the so called 'events' ('event' = index changes during the day), e.g., 'no significant changes', 'fluctuations', 'increase' etc., or the tendencies (e.g., index behavior during the first hour after the trades opening). After that the NLG module takes the event as input and generates a text according to the changes the indexes had.

In the next two subsections we illustrate how these modules function.

3.1 Analysis module

The analysis module uses the data on indexes values to detect the behavior the indexes had during one particular period of time. For the morning news generation we take the previous trading day data and the data on the first hour of the trades, for the evening news — the current day data. As it was meantioned before the stock news generation in our case demands detecting tendencies and events. Determining tendencies is retalively easy, one compares the difference between two index values: the opening value and the last value. The tendencies could be for example 'increase', 'decrease' etc. Determining events is a more complicated procedure, also the events can have a more complex structure than the tendencies. We dis-

tinguish simple events like 'increase', 'decrease' 'fluctuations' and also such events as 'significant increase & no changes' or 'increase & insignificant decrease' and other similar compound events. For events determination we use the following algorithm:

1. *Check if the index fluctuated.*

We check it by calculating the *Adjusted* R^2 value, if it appears to be less than 0.5 then we claim that the index has fluctuated.

2. *Check if there are intervals without any significant changes.*

For each interval $[t_1, \ t_2]$ we calculate the evaluative function by using this formula:

$$E = \alpha(t_1 - t_2) + \frac{\beta}{\sigma_{1,2}^2 + 10^{-4}} \ ,$$

where $\sigma_{1,2}$ — standard deviation in the interval, α, β — coefficients. Thus, the bigger the interval is, the more is the evaluative function value and the less the index fluctuates, the more is the evaluative function value.

3. *Fit the polynomials of degrees 2 and 3 to the index values data.*

4. *Choose the best approximation.*

Since we had detected the interval with no significant changes and fit the polynomials, we choose the approximation that best of all corresponds to the index behavior. If the interval with no significant changes is between 1/3 and 1/2 of the whole trading day length and it is located in the first or the second half of the day, then we choose this approximation. Otherwise, we should choose between the two polynomials. Most of the cases are well described with the help of quadratic polynomial, so we have to determine if the cubic polynomial is needed or not. To acomplish that one should find the inflection point of the cubic polynomial and the difference between the *Adjusted* R^2 values of the polynomials.

5. *Apply the rules to determine the event.*

If the check for the intervals with no significant changes was positive, then the resulting 'event' will consist of 'no significant change' part and 'increase/decrease etc.' part, e.g., 'no significant change & significant decrease' or 'increase & no significant change'. If the quadratic polynomial was chosen as a suitable approximation, then one will need such parameters as the sign of the x^2 coefficient, the vertex location on the time axis and the threshold crossing (if the changes exceeded 2% relative to the opening then we call such changes significant and it affects the event) to determine the event. If the cubic polynomial was chosen as a suitable approximation, then one will need to know the the sign of the x^3 coefficient to determine the event.

By the means of this algorithm one can determine different types of index changes both simple like 'decrease', 'increase', 'fluctuations' and compound changes like 'no significant changes & increase'. The information about the index changes is further used by the NLG module for news generation.

3.2 NLG module

In this section we describe the NLG process in our system. This module uses text layouts, rules, sentence templates and financial lexicon that was collected during the work with media texts. In the result we get short texts like this one below.

(1)
Russian
Segodnya torgi prohodili v krasnoy zone. Utrom indeks MMVB nachal torgi ponizheniem i prodolzhal ustremlyat'sya vniz. V to zhe vremya, ruhnuv utrom, indeks RTS prodolzhil sil'noe padenie. Tak indeks MMVB ponizilsya na 0.39% do otmetki v 1748 punktov, a indeks RTS — snizilsya na 4.4% i dostig 804 punktov. Ob"em torgov po itogam dnya sostavil 700 millionov dollarov SSHA.

English translation
Today the trades ran in the red zone. In the morning MOEX index started to reduce and continued its lowering. At the same time RTSI fell and proceeded to decrease. So MOEX lost 0.39 % and made up 1748 points, RTSI fell by 4.4 % and reached the grade of 804 points. The volume of the trading section was 700 millions of dollars.

First of all the program takes an appropriate text layout (morning/evening). In traditional descriptions of NLG architecture, as in (Reiter et al., 2000) or (Martin and Jurafsky, 2000),

one of the steps in the implementation is the macro planning. In some NLG the systems it is done authomatically but in our system the macro planning appears to be predetermined. Then the program fills in the positions with different sentence templates. For each position there are more than one suitable template. The templates are clauses with some constituents missing. Some of them have more slots, some of them less, depending on how much variance is needed. Most of the templates are independent clauses, but some of them turn out to be the constituents of one compound sentence in the result. Here are some examples of the templates the program uses for generation.

(2) [timeExpr] [subject] began to [predicate].

(3) [timeExpr] MOEX index [predicate] [value]% to [value] points, RTSI index [predicate] [value]% to [value] points.

(4) a.   [timeExpr] MOEX index [predicate] [value] % to [value] points.
b.   , [link] RTSI index [predicate] [value] % to [value] points.

In examples (2) and (3) we presented the templates for independent clauses, but in (4) there are two clauses connected by the linking word. The words in the square brackets represent the missing constituents or the slots of the templates.

The next step is filling in the slots in the templates with the words from our lexicon. The information about the types of index changes, or the events, affected the contents and the structure of the lexicon (both predicates and connective words) that is used by the program. There are groups of lexemes which characterize the changes and correspond to particular events. For example there are such groups as 'negative change predicates', e.g., *to fall*, *to decrease*, 'positive change predicates', e.g., *to rise*, *to increase*, 'no change predicates', e.g., *to remain constant*, etc. There are also such groups of words like 'nouns of change' related to the verbs, e.g., *rise*, *growth*, and 'intensifiers', e.g., *considerably*, *a lot*, etc.

Since we generate the news about two indexes which are indepent and can have different changes on the same day, it appears to be highly important to use plenty of connectives to provide the flu-

ency to the texts. When the sentence templates had
been already chosen and the most of the slots were
filled in, the program applies the rules of templates
combining. For example, if in the template (4a)
the predicate is 'to increase (by)' and in (4b) it is
'to fall (by)', then the program chooses the adversative conjunction as a link for these clauses. In
gerenal the choice of the connectives depends on
the correlation of changes that two indexes demonstrate. It is taken into account if the indexes have
the same change tendencies or they differ in their
behavior and how much differ in it.

When all the previous steps are finished the program does the post-processing such as adding the
punctuation marks and capitalisation where it is
needed.

4   Evaluation

The system evaluation was divided into two
stages, because the modules were evaluated separately.

The analysis module evaluation was done in the
following way. For 100 data samples of index
changes during the day we automatically determined their events and then manualy checked how
many of these were determined correctly. The percentage of the right answers we got was 87%.

The NLG module was evaluated both manually
and automatically using the BLEU metric (Papineni et al., 2002). For the manual evaluation we
took 100 generated texts. These texts were rated
according to the following scale: 2 — 'fluent', 1
— 'understandable', 0 — 'disfluent'. It turned out
that 61% of the texts were fluent, 28% were understandable and 5% were disfluent. The BLEU
value appeared to be 0.66, for the calculation we
used 70 gold standard sentences and 50 automatically generated sentences that describe the index
changes. We decided to pick them for evaluation
because unlike the other sentences in the news the
sentences about changes have a high level of variation. We also admit the lack of gold standard material might have affected the BLEU results.

5   Acknowledgements

I would like to thank Alexei Nesterenko, PhD, for
his advice, help and encouragement while I was
doing the math for this research, I am also very
thankful to Anastasia Bonch-Osmolovskaya, PhD,
for her support and help during the whole time I
worked on this paper and to Andrei Babitsky for

his expert opinion on what the output news texts
should be like.

References

Blake Howald, Ravi Kondadadi, and Frank Schilder.
2013. Domain adaptable semantic clustering in
statistical nlg. In *Proceedings of the 10th International Conference on Computational Semantics
(IWCS 2013)*, pages 143–154.

Karen Kukich. 1983. Design of a knowledge-based
report generator. In *Proceedings of the 21st annual
meeting on Association for Computational Linguistics*, pages 145–150. Association for Computational
Linguistics.

James H Martin and Daniel Jurafsky. 2000. Speech
and language processing. *International Edition*,
710.

Kishore Papineni, Salim Roukos, Todd Ward, and Wei-
Jing Zhu. 2002. Bleu: a method for automatic
evaluation of machine translation. In *Proceedings of
the 40th annual meeting on association for computational linguistics*, pages 311–318. Association for
Computational Linguistics.

Ehud Reiter, Robert Dale, and Zhiwei Feng. 2000.
Building natural language generation systems, volume 33. MIT Press.

Ilya Sutskever, James Martens, and Geoffrey E Hinton. 2011. Generating text with recurrent neural
networks. In *Proceedings of the 28th International
Conference on Machine Learning (ICML-11)*, pages
1017–1024.

Kees Van Deemter, Emiel Krahmer, and Mariët Theune. 2005. Real versus template-based natural language generation: A false opposition? *Computational Linguistics*, 31(1):15–24.

Content Selection as Semantic-Based Ontology Exploration

Laura Perez-Beltrachini
CNRS/LORIA
Nancy (France)
laura.perez@loria.fr

Claire Gardent
CNRS/LORIA
Nancy (France)
claire.gardent@loria.fr

Anselme Revuz
I.U.T. Blagnac
Toulouse (France)
anselme.revuz@gmail.com

Saptarashmi Bandyopadhyay
IIEST
Shibpur (India)
saptarashmicse@gmail.com

1   Introduction

Natural Language (NL) based access to information contained in Knowledge Bases (KBs) has been tackled by approaches following different paradigms. One strand of research deals with the task of ontology-based data access and data exploration (Franconi et al., 2010; Franconi et al., 2011). This type of approach relies on two pillar components. The first one is an ontology describing the underlying domain with a set of reasoning based query construction operations. This component guides the lay user in the formulation of a KB query by proposing alternatives for query expansion. The second is a Natural Language Generation (NLG) system to hide the details of the formal query language to the user. Our ultimate goal is the automatic creation of a corpus of KB queries for development and evaluation of NLG systems.

The task we address is the following. Given an ontology $\mathcal{K}$, automatically select from $\mathcal{K}$ descriptions q which yield sensible user queries. The difficulty lies in the fact that ontologies often omit important *disjointness axioms* and adequate *domain* or *range restrictions* (Rector et al., 2004; Poveda-Villalón et al., 2012). For instance, the toy ontology shown in Figure 1 licences the meaningless query in (1). This happens because there is no disjointness axiom between the Song and Rectangular concepts and/or because the domain of the marriedTo relation is not restricted to persons.

(1)   *Who are the rectangular songs married to a person?*
Song $\sqcap$ Rectangular $\sqcap$ $\exists$ marriedTo.Person

$$\top \sqsubseteq \forall\, \mathsf{marriedTo.Person}$$
$$\mathsf{Person} \sqsubseteq \top$$
$$\mathsf{Song} \sqsubseteq \top$$
$$\mathsf{Rectangular} \sqsubseteq \mathsf{Shape}$$

Figure 1: Toy ontology.

In this work, we explore to what extent vector space models can help to improve the coherence of automatically formulated KB queries. These models are learnt from large corpora and provide general shared common semantic knowledge. Such models have been proposed for related tasks. For example, (Freitas et al., 2014) proposes a distributional semantic approach for the exploration of paths in a knowledge graph and (Corman et al., 2015) uses distributional semantics for spotting common sense inconsistencies in large KBs.

Our approach draws on the fact that natural language is used to name elements, i.e. concepts and relations, in ontologies (Mellish and Sun, 2006). Hence, the idea is to exploit lexical semantics to detect incoherent query expansions during the automatic query formulation process. Following ideas from the work in (Kruszewski and Baroni, 2015; Van de Cruys, 2014), our approach uses word vector representations as lexical semantic resources. We train two semantic "compatibility" models, namely DISCOMP and DRCOMP . The first one will model incompatibility between concepts in a candidate query expansion and the second incompatibility between concepts and candidate properties.

2   Query language and operations

Following (cf. (Guagliardo, 2009)) a KB query is a labelled tree where edges are labelled with a relation name and nodes are labelled with a variable and a non-empty set of concept names from the ontology.

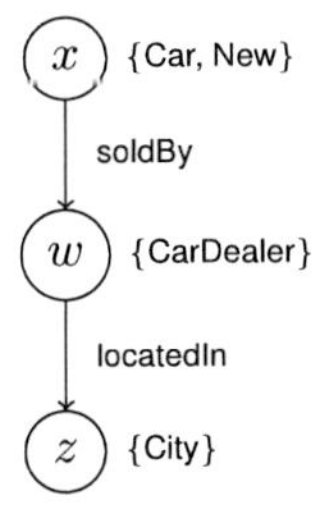

The query construction process starts from the initial KB query with a single node. The four operations (cf. (Guagliardo, 2009) for a formal definition of the operations) available for iteratively refining the KB query are: *add* for

Proceedings of the 2nd International Workshop on Natural Language Generation and the Semantic Web (WebNLG), pages 41–45,
Edinburgh, Scotland, September 6th, 2016. ©2016 Association for Computational Linguistics

the addition of new concepts and relations; *substitution* for replacing a portion of the query with a more general, specific or compatible concept; *deletion* for removing a selected part of the query; and *weaken* for making the query as general as possible. A sequence of query formulation steps illustrating these operations is shown in Figure 2.

I am looking for something. (Initial request)

... for a new car. (Substitution)

... for a new car sold by a car dealer. (Add relation)

... for a new car, a coupé sold by a car dealer. (Add concept)

... for a new car sold by a car dealer. (Deletion)

... for a car sold by a car dealer. (Weaken)

Figure 2: Query formulation sequence.

3 Extracting KB queries

To automatically select queries from a KB, we randomise the application of the *add* and operation. That is, starting from a query tree with one node, the operation is iteratively applied at a randomly selected node up to a maximum number of steps[1]. The *add* operation divides in *add compatible concepts* and *add compatible relations* (cf. (Guagliardo, 2009)). Given a node n labelled with concept s, the first one will add another concept label s' (e.g., Car and New in the example query tree in Section 2), the second will attach a relation and its range (p, o) to the node (e.g., (CarDealer, locatedIn, City)).

The add operation picks up a concept (relation) from a list of candidate concepts (relations) to expand the current query. These candidates are computed using reasoning operations on the query build so far and the underlying ontology. As discussed in Section 1, the lack of axioms in the ontology will enable the inference and the selection of incoherent candidate content such as (Song, Rectangular) and (Song, marriedTo, Person).

To filter out incoherent suggestions made by the add operations we propose the following models[2].

Concept compatibility model (DISCOMP). As explained in (Kruszewski and Baroni, 2015), distributional semantic representations provide models for semantic relatedness and have shown good performance in many lexical semantic tasks (Baroni et al., 2014). While they model semantic re-

latedness, for instance, *car* and *tyre* are related concepts, they fail to capture the notion of semantic compatibility. That is, there is no thing that can be both a *car* and a *tyre* at the same time. Thus, they propose a Neural Network (NN) model that learns semantic characteristics of concepts classifying them as (in)compatible. We adapt their best performing model, namely 2L-interaction, for our task of detecting whether two ontology concepts (s, s') are incompatible.

Selectional compatibility model (DRCOMP). Selectional constraints concern the semantic type imposed by predicates to the arguments they take. For instance, the predicate *sell* will impose the constraint for its subjects to be, for instance, of type Organisation or Person. Thus, it would be acceptable to say *A car dealer sells new cars* while it would be rare to say *A tyre sells new cars*.

Our idea is to apply the notion of selectional preferences to ontology relations and the concepts they can be combined with. That is, whether a candidate relation p to be attached to a node labelled with concept s, i.e. forming the triple $(s, p, o)^3$, is a plausible candidate. Along the lines of the work in (Van de Cruys, 2014), we train a NN model to predict (in)compatible subject concept - relation (s, p) pairs[4].

4 Experimental setup

Both models use the best performing word vectors available at http://clic.cimec.unitn. it/composes/semantic-vectors.html (Baroni et al., 2014).

DISCOMP **dataset.** This dataset consists of compatible and incompatible example pairs. We extract them in the following way. We combine a set of manually annotated pairs with a set of automatically extracted ones.

As manually annotated examples, we use the dataset of (Kruszewski and Baroni, 2015) plus additional examples extracted from the results of dif-

---

[1]A parameter to the random query generation process.

[2]Note that another alternative would be to use the models we introduce to help with the enrichment ontologies.

[3]Note that the concept o taking the object argument place corresponds to the range of the relation. Thus, at this stage, we do not attempt to model relation object concept (in)compatibility.

[4]The architecture of our NN is similar to that proposed by (Van de Cruys, 2014). However, rather than using a ranking loss function, we approximate this by training the network with a hinge loss function over labels (-1,1). Another difference is that our input embedding layer is static and initialised with pre-trained vectors.

ferent runs of the *add* operation which were annotated manually. These provide 7764 examples.

In addition, we automatically extracted compatible and incompatible pairs of concepts from existing ontologies. For incompatible pairs (5273 examples), we extracted definitions of disjoint axioms from 52 ontologies crawled from the web and from YAGO (Suchanek et al., 2008). The compatible pairs (57968 examples) were extracted from YAGO using the class membership of individuals. We assume that if an instance a is defined as a member of the class A and of the class B at the same time then both classes are compatible.

The final dataset contains 71918 instances. We take 80% for training and the rest for testing.

DRCOMP **dataset.** We automatically extract subject-predicate pairs (s, p) from two different sources, namely `nsubj` dependencies from parsed sentences and `domain` restrictions in ontologies.

For the extraction of pairs from text, we use the ukWaCKy corpus (Baroni et al., 2009), we call this subset of pairs *ukWaCKy.SP*, and the Matoll corpus (Walter et al., 2013), call it the *WikiDBP.SP* subset. Both corpora contain dependency parsed sentences. In addition, the Matoll corpus provides annotations linking entities mentioned in the text with DBPedia entities. For the first *SP* dataset, we take the head and dependent participating in `nsubj` dependency relations as training pairs (s, p). For the second *SP* dataset, we use the DBPedia annotations associated to `nsubj` dependents. That is, we create (s, p) pairs where the s component rather than being the head entity mention, it is the DBPedia concept to which this entity belongs to. We do this by using the DBPedia entity annotations present in the corpus. For instance, given the dependency `nsubj(Stan Kenton, winning)`, because *Stan Kenton* is annotated with the DBPedia entity `http://dbpedia.org/resource/Stan_Kenton` and this entity is defined to be of type Person and Artist, among others, we can create (s, p) pairs such as $(person, winning)$ and $(artist, winning)$.

For the pairs based on ontology definitions, we use the 52 ontologies crawled from the web. We call this subset of pairs *KB.SP*.

For training the model, we generate negative instances by corrupting the extracted data. For each (s, p) pair in the dataset we generate an (s', p) pair where s' is not seen occurring with p in the training corpus. The final dataset contains 610522 training instances (30796 from *ukWaCKy.SP*, 571564 from *WikiDBP.SP* and 8162 from *KB.SP*). We take out 600 cases, 300 from *ukWaCKy.SP* and 300 from *KB.SP*, for testing the model on specific text and KB pairs.

5 Evaluation

We separately evaluate the performance of each model in a held out testing set. Table 1 shows the results for the DISCOMP model. Table 2 shows the results obtained when evaluating the DRCOMP model. Both models perform well in the intrinsic evaluation.

Test dataset	Accuracy
(Kruszewski and Baroni, 2015)	0.72
DISCOMP	0.98

Table 1: Results reported by (Kruszewski and Baroni, 2015) and results obtained with the DISCOMP model.

	Test dataset	Accuracy
Emb. + NN	ukWaCKy.SP	0.69
	KB.SP	0.77

Table 2: Results after (Emb.+NN) training with the union of the *ukWaCKy.SP*, *WikiDBP.SP* and *KB.SP* training sets. Note that if we train only with the *ukWaCKy.SP* training set and we evaluate with the *ukWaCKy.SP* testing set we get an accuracy of 0.86 which is similar to the results reported in (Van de Cruys, 2014).

We also asses the performance of the models on the task of meaningful query generation. We run the random query generation process over 5 ontologies of different domains, namely cars, travel, wines, conferences and human disabilities. At each query expansion operation, we apply the models to the sets of candidate concepts or relations. We compare the DISCOMP and DRCOMP models with a baseline cosine similarity (COS) score[5]. For this score we use GloVe (Pennington et al., 2014) word embeddings and simple addition for composing multiword concept and relation names. We use a threshold of 0.3 that was determined empirically[6]. During the query generation process, we registered the candidate sets as well as

---

[5]For the case of add candidate relations, the COS model checks for semantic relatedness between a subject concept and the relation and between the subject concept and the object concept, i.e. (s,p) and (s,o)

[6]We compare the COS baseline plus a threshold of 0.3

	addRelation		addCompatible	
	Cos	DRCOMP	Cos	DISCOMP
P	0.51	0.67	0.90	0.88
R	0.30	0.33	0.41	0.85
F	0.38	0.44	0.56	0.87
S	0.79	0.88	0.77	0.46
A	0.59	0.65	0.47	0.78

Table 3: Precision (P), recall (R), F-measure (F), specificity (S) and accuracy (A) results for the DISCOMP , DRCOMP and Cos on the add compatible relation (addRelation) and add compatible concept (addCompatible) query expansion operations.

the predictions of the models. In total, we collected 67 candidate sets corresponding to the add compatible relation query extension and 39 to the add compatible operation. The candidate sets were manually annotated with (in)compatibility human judgements. We use these sets as gold standard to compute precision, recall, f-measure and specificity measures on the task of detecting incompatible candidates as well as the accuracy of the models. Figure 3 shows one example for each of the query expansion operations, the annotated candidates and the predictions done by each of the models (only incompatibles are shown).

Table 3 shows the results. Unsurprisingly, given the quite strong similarity threshold used for the Cos baseline, we observe that it has good precision at spotting incompatible candidates though quite low recall. In contrast, as shown by the f-measure values the compatibility models seem to achieve a better performance compromise for these measures. We include the specificity measure as an indicative of the ability of the models to avoid false alarms, that is, to avoid predicting a candidate as incompatible when it was not.

6 Conclusions and future work

We applied two compatibility models to get around the lack of disjointness and domain restrictions in ontologies and facilitate the (semi-) automatic generation of a large set of sensible user KB queries. These compatibility models were previously proposed for two semantic tasks. One for term compatibility (Kruszewski and Baroni, 2015) and the other for selectional preference modelling (Van de Cruys, 2014). We automatically created training datasets from several text and knowl-

[Add compatible concept] [Assistant]
[CANDIDATES] [Author:0, SubjectArea:1, Administrator:0, Member_PC:0, Science_Worker:0, Volunteer:0, Scholar:0, Regular:1, Student:0]
[Cos] [Member_PC]
[DISCOMP] [SubjectArea, Volunteer, Regular]

[Add relation] [Poster]
[CANDIDATES] [dealsWith:0, writtenBy:0]
[Cos] [dealsWith]
[DRCOMP] [ ]

Figure 3: Example of gold standard annotations for the add compatible concept and relation operations and predictions done by the different systems.

edge base resources with the intention of providing more adequate training signal for our specific task.

As future work, we aim at running a larger task based extrinsic evaluation of these models. We plan to generate a set of KB queries, verbalise them using techniques proposed in (Gardent and Perez-Beltrachini, 2016; Perez-Beltrachini and Gardent, 2016) and ask for human judgements about meaningfulness of the generated queries. In this larger evaluation, we plan to test the models on larger general purpose KBs such as DBPedia.

Further work for improving on the current results could explore the adaptation of the models to specific domain vocabularies and the use of better composition modelling for multiwords concepts and relations.

Acknowledgements

We thank the French National Research Agency for funding the research presented in this paper in the context of the WebNLG project. We would also like to thank Sebastian Walter for kindly providing us with the MATOLL corpus and the volunteer annotator for contributing to the evaluation.

References

Marco Baroni, Silvia Bernardini, Adriano Ferraresi, and Eros Zanchetta. 2009. The wacky wide web: a collection of very large linguistically processed web-crawled corpora. *Language resources and evaluation*, 43(3):209–226.

Marco Baroni, Georgiana Dinu, and Germán Kruszewski. 2014. Don't count, predict! a systematic comparison of context-counting vs. context-predicting semantic vectors. In *ACL (1)*, pages 238–247.

---

and the Cos baseline with 0.5. Setting this threshold is really a trade off between precision and recall. The use of the 0.5 threshold resulted in rejection of most of the candidates including compatible ones.

Julien Corman, Laure Vieu, and Nathalie Aussenac-Gilles. 2015. Distributional semantics for ontology verification. In *Proceedings of the Fourth Joint Conference on Lexical and Computational Semantics*, pages 30–39, Denver, Colorado, June. Association for Computational Linguistics.

Enrico Franconi, Paolo Guagliardo, and Marco Trevisan. 2010. Quelo: a NL-based intelligent query interface. In *Pre-Proceedings of the Second Workshop on Controlled Natural Languages*, volume 622.

Enrico Franconi, Paolo Guagliardo, Marco Trevisan, and Sergio Tessaris. 2011. Quelo: an Ontology-Driven Query Interface. In *Description Logics*.

André Freitas, João Carlos Pereira da Silva, Edward Curry, and Paul Buitelaar. 2014. A distributional semantics approach for selective reasoning on commonsense graph knowledge bases. In *Natural Language Processing and Information Systems*, pages 21–32. Springer.

Claire Gardent and Laura Perez-Beltrachini. 2016. A Statistical, Grammar-Based Approach to Micro-Planning. *Computational Linguistics*.

Paolo Guagliardo. 2009. Theoretical foundations of an ontology-based visual tool for query formulation support. Master's thesis, KRDB Research Centre, Free University of Bozen-Bolzano, October.

Germán Kruszewski and Marco Baroni. 2015. So similar and yet incompatible: Toward automated identification of semantically compatible words. pages 964–969.

Chris Mellish and Xiantang Sun. 2006. The semantic web as a linguistic resource: Opportunities for natural language generation. *Knowledge-Based Systems*, 19(5):298–303.

Jeffrey Pennington, Richard Socher, and Christopher D. Manning. 2014. Glove: Global vectors for word representation. In *Empirical Methods in Natural Language Processing (EMNLP)*, pages 1532–1543.

Laura Perez-Beltrachini and Claire Gardent. 2016. Learning Embeddings to lexicalise RDF Properties. In **SEM 2016: The Fifth Joint Conference on Lexical and Computational Semantics*, Berlin, Germany.

María Poveda-Villalón, Mari Carmen Suárez-Figueroa, and Asunción Gómez-Pérez. 2012. Validating ontologies with oops! In *International Conference on Knowledge Engineering and Knowledge Management*, pages 267–281. Springer.

Alan Rector, Nick Drummond, Matthew Horridge, Jeremy Rogers, Holger Knublauch, Robert Stevens, Hai Wang, and Chris Wroe. 2004. Owl pizzas: Practical experience of teaching owl-dl: Common errors & common patterns. In *In Proc. of EKAW 2004*, pages 63–81. Springer.

Fabian M Suchanek, Gjergji Kasneci, and Gerhard Weikum. 2008. Yago: A large ontology from wikipedia and wordnet. *Web Semantics: Science, Services and Agents on the World Wide Web*, 6(3):203–217.

Tim Van de Cruys. 2014. A neural network approach to selectional preference acquisition. In *Proceedings of the 2014 Conference on Empirical Methods in Natural Language Processing (EMNLP)*, pages 26–35.

Sebastian Walter, Christina Unger, and Philipp Cimiano. 2013. A corpus-based approach for the induction of ontology lexica. In *Natural Language Processing and Information Systems*, pages 102–113. Springer.

ReadME Generation from an OWL Ontology
Describing NLP Tools

Driss Sadoun, Satenik Mkhitaryan, Damien Nouvel, Mathieu Valette
ERTIM, INALCO, Paris, France
firstname.lastname@inalco.fr

Abstract

The paper deals with the generation of *ReadME* files from an ontology-based description of NLP tool. *ReadME* files are structured and organised according to properties defined in the ontology. One of the problem is being able to deal with multilingual generation of texts. To do so, we propose to map the ontology elements to multilingual knowledge defined in a SKOS ontology.

1 Introduction

A *ReadMe* file is a simple and short written document that is commonly distributed along with a computer software, forming part of its documentation. It is generally written by the developer and is supposed to contain basic and crucial information that the user reads before installing and running the software.

Existing NLP software may range from unstable prototypes to industrial applications. Many of them are developed by researchers, in the framework of temporary projects (training, PhD theses, funded projects). As their use is often restricted to their developers, they do not always meet *Information technology* (IT) requirements in terms of documentation and reusability. This is especially the case for under-resourced languages, which are often developed by researchers and released without standard documentation, or written fully or partly in the developer's native language.

Providing a clear *ReadMe* file is essential for effective software distribution and use: a confusing one could prevent the user from using the software. However, there is no well established guidelines or good practices for writing a *ReadMe*.

In this paper we propose an ontology-based approach for the generation of ordered and structured *ReadMe* files for NLP tools. The ontology defines a meta-data model built based on a joint study of NLP tool documentation practices and existing meta-data model for language resources (cf. section 2). Translation functions (TFs) for different languages (currently eight) are associated to ontology properties characterising NLP tools. These *TFs* are defined within the *Simple Knowledge Organization System (SKOS)* (cf. section 2.2). The ontology is filled via an on-line platform by NLP experts speaking different languages. Each expert describes the NLP tools processing the languages he speaks (cf. section 3). A *ReadMe* file is then generated in different languages for each tool described within the ontology (cf. section 3). Figure 1 depicts the whole process of multilingual *ReadMe* generation.

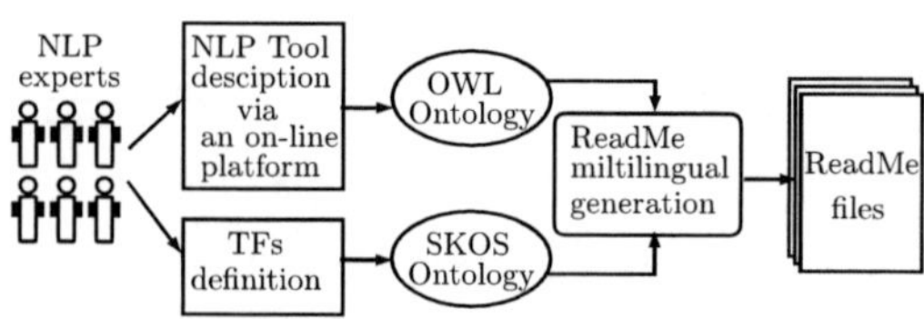

Figure 1: ReadMe generation process

2 NLP tools ontology

This work takes place in the framework of the project *MultiTal* which aims at making NLP tool descriptions available through an online platform, containing factual information and verbose descriptions that should ease installation and use of considered NLP tools. This project involves numerous NLP experts

Proceedings of the 2nd International Workshop on Natural Language Generation and the Semantic Web (WebNLG), pages 46–49,
Edinburgh, Scotland, September 6th, 2016. ©2016 Association for Computational Linguistics

in diverse languages, currently *Arabic, English, French, Hindi, Japanese, Mandarin Chinese, Russian, Ukrainian* and *Tibetan*. Our objective is to take advantage of the NLP experts knowledge both to retrieve NLP tools in their languages and to generate multilingual *ReadMe* files for the retrieved NLP tools. A first step to reach this goal is to propose a conceptual model whose elements are as much independent as possible from the language. Then, associate to each conceptual element, a lexicalisation for each targeted language.

2.1 Ontology conceptualisation

In order to conceptualise an ontology that structures and standardises the description of NLP tools we proceeded to a joint study of:

- Documentation for various NLP tools processing aforementioned languages that have been installed and closely tested;

- A large collection (around ten thousands) of structured *ReadMe* in the *Markdown* format, crawled from *GitHub* repositories;

- Meta-data models for Language Resources (LR) as the CMDI (Broeder et al., 2012) or META-SHARE meta-data model ontology (McCrae et al., 2015).

This study gave us guidelines to define bundles of properties sharing a similar semantic. For example, properties referring to the affiliation of the tool (as *hasAuthor, hasLaboratory* or *hasProjet*), to its installation or its usage.

We distinguish two levels of meta-data: 1) a *mandatory level* providing basic elements that constitute a *ReadMe* file and 2) a *non-mandatory level* that contains additional information as relations to other tools, fields or methods. These latter serve tools' indexation within the on-line platform.

Figure 2 details the major bundles of properties that we conceptualized to describe an NLP tool. The processed languages are defined within the bundle *Task*. Indeed, an NLP tool may have different tasks which may apply to different languages.

As our ambition is to propose pragmatic descriptions detailing the possible installation and execution procedures, we particularly focused on the decomposition of these procedures into atomic actions.

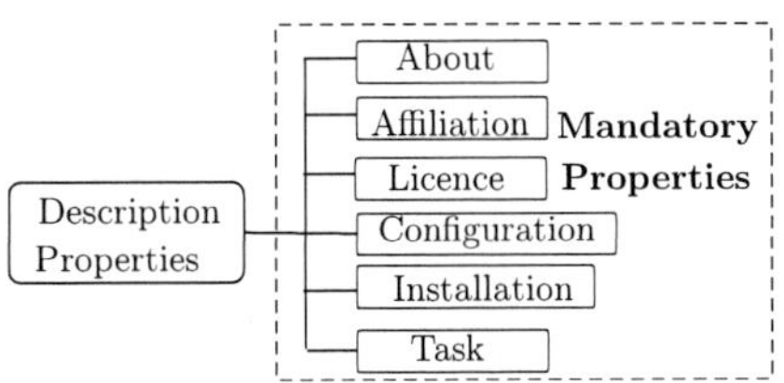

Figure 2: Bundles of properties representing ReadMe sections

2.2 Multilingual translation functions

Within the ontology, NLP tools are characterised by their properties. Values allocated to these properties are as much as possible independent of the language (date of creation and last update, developer or license names, operating system information, ...). Hence, what needs to be lexicalised is the semantic of each defined property. Each NLP expert associate to each property a translation functions (*TFs*) that formalise the lexical formulation of the property in the language he speaks. *TFs* are defined once for each language. The amount of work have not exceeded half a day per language to associate *TFs* to the around eighty properties of the ontology. In order to ensure a clean separation between the conceptual and the lexical layer, *TFs* are defined within a *SKOS* ontology. The *SKOS* ontology structure is automatically created from the OWL ontology. Thus, adding a new language essentially consists in adding within *SKOS TFs* in that particular language to each OWL property. Translation functions are of two kinds:

1. $P(V_1) \rightsquigarrow\ * V_1\ *@lang$

2. $P(V_1,V_2) \rightsquigarrow\ * V_1 * V_2 *$ or $* V_2 * V_1 *\ @lang$

with P a property, * a set of words that can be empty, V_1, V_2 values of the property P and *@lang* an OWL language tag that determines the language in which the property is lexicalised. Below, two examples of *tranlation functions* for Japanese that have been associated to the properties *authorFirstName* and *download*.

- $authorFirstName(V_1) \rightsquigarrow$ 作成者名: V_1 @jp

- $download(V_1,V_2) \rightsquigarrow V_2$ から V_1 をダウンロードする。@jp

3 Natural language generation of multilingual *ReadMe* files

In our framework, each NLP expert finds, installs and uses available NLP tools processing the language he speaks. Then, he describes every tool that runs correctly via an on-line platform connected to the ontology (cf. Figure 1). Elements of description do not only come from an existing *ReadMe* as if they exist, they are rarely exhaustive. Hence, experts also gather tool information from the web and during installing and testing each tool.

At this step, the *OWL* ontology is filled and the translated functions of each property are defined within the *SKOS* ontology. Our aim is to generate ordered and structured *ReadMe* files in different languages. To do so, we use *Natural language generation (NLG)* techniques adapted to the Semantic Web (also named *Ontology verbalisation*) (Staykova, 2014; Bouayad-Agha et al., 2014; Cojocaru and Trăuşan Matu, 2015; Keet and Khumalo, 2016). *NLG* can be divided in several tasks (Reiter and Dale, 2000; Staykova, 2014). Our approach currently includes: *content selection, document structuring, knowledge aggregation*, and *lexicalisation*. The use of more advanced tasks as *referring expression aggregation, linguistic realisation* and *structure realisation* is in our perspectives.

3.1 Ontology content selection and structuring

Unlike the majority of *ontology verbalisation* approaches, we do not intend to verbalise the whole content of the ontology. We simply verbalize properties and their values that characterise a pertinent information that have to appear in a *ReadMe* file. The concerned properties are those which belong to the *mandatory level* (cf. section 2.1).

The structure of *ReadMe* files is formalized within the ontology. First, *ReadMe* files are organised in sections based on bundles of properties defined in the ontology (cf. Figure 2). Within each section, the order of property is predefined. Both installation and execution procedures are decomposed to their atomic actions. These actions are automatically numbered according to their order of execution (cf. Figure 3). Different installation and execution procedures may exist according the operat-

ing system (Linux, Windows, ...), architecture (32bits, 64bites, 86bits, ...), language platform (JAVA 8, Python 3, ...) and so on. As well, execution procedures depend on tasks the NLP tool performs and the languages it processes. Thus, each procedure is distinguished and its information grouped under its heading. Moreover, execution procedures are also ordered as an NLP tool may have to perform tasks in a particular ordered sequence. This structuring is part of the ontology conceptualisation. It consists in defining property and sub-property relations and in associating a sequence number to each property that has to be lexicalised.

3.2 Ontology content aggregation and lexicalisation

Following the heuristics proposed in (Androutsopoulos et al., 2014) and (Cojocaru and Trăuşan Matu, 2015) to obtain concise text, OWL property values are aggregated when they characterise the same object. For example, if an *execution procedure* (ep_i) has two values for *operating system* (ex : Linux and Mac) then the two values are merged as the following below:

$hasOS(ep_i,\text{Linux}) \wedge hasOS(ep_i,\text{Mac})$
$\Rightarrow hasOS(ep_i,\text{Linux and Mac})$

The last step consists in *property lexicalisation*. While a number of approaches rely on ontology elements' names and labels (often in English) to infer a lexicalisation (Bontcheva, 2005; SUN and MELLISH, 2006; Williams et al., 2011), in our approach, the lexicalisation of properties depend only on their translation functions. During the ontology verbalisation, each targeted language is processed one after the other. The *TF* of encountered properties for the current language is retrieved and used to lexicalise the property. Property values are considered as variables of the *TFs*. They are not translated as we ensure that they are as much as possible independent of the language. Figure 3 gives an example of two installation procedures for the NLP tool *Jieba* that processes Chinese. In this example, actions are lexicalised in English. Furthermore, the lexicalised command lines appear in between brackets.

As a result of this generation, all *ReadMe* files have the same structure, organisation and, as much as possible, level of detail, especially regarding installation and execution procedures which represent the key information for a tool usage. The resulted texts are simple which suits a *ReadMe*. However, it could be valuable to use more advanced NLG techniques as *referring expression aggregation, linguistic realisation* and *structure realisation* to produce more less simplified natural language texts.

Procedure name: *wget - ubuntu*

1- *download* jieba-0.38.zip *via wget* (wget https://pypi.python.org/packages/f6/86 /9e721cc52075a07b7d07eb12bcb5dde771d35332a 3dae1e14ae4290a197a/jieba-0.38.zip)
2- *unzip* jieba-0.38.zip (unzip jieba-0.38.zip)
3- *go to the directory* jieba-0.38 (cd jieba-0.38/)
4- *type the command:* python setup.py install

Procedure name: *pip - ubuntu*

1 - *type the command:* sudo pip install jieba

Figure 3: Two installation procedures of the NLP tool *Jieba* lexicalised in English.

4   Conclusion

We proposed an ontology-based approach for generating simple, structured and organised ReadMe files in different languages. *Readme* structuring and lexicalisation is guided by the ontology properties and their associated *translation functions* for the targeted languages. The generated *ReadMes* are intended to be accessible via an on-line platform. This platform documents in several languages NLP tools processing different languages. In a near future, we plan to evaluate the complexity for end-users of different level of expertise to install and execute NLP tools using our generated *ReadMe* files. We also hope that, as a side-product, the proposed conceptualisation may provide a starting point to establish guidelines and best practices that NLP tool documentation often lacks, especially for under-resourced languages.

References

Ion Androutsopoulos, Gerasimos Lampouras, and Dimitrios Galanis. 2014. Generating natural language descriptions from OWL ontologies: the naturalowl system. *CoRR*, abs/1405.6164.

Kalina Bontcheva, 2005. *The Semantic Web: Research and Applications: Second European Semantic Web Conference, ESWC*, chapter Generating Tailored Textual Summaries from Ontologies, pages 531–545.

Nadjet Bouayad-Agha, Gerard Casamayor, and Leo Wanner. 2014. Natural language generation in the context of the semantic web. *Semantic Web*, 5(6):493–513.

Daan Broeder, Dieter Van Uytvanck, Maria Gavrilidou, Thorsten Trippel, and Menzo Windhouwer. 2012. Standardizing a component metadata infrastructure. In *LREC*, pages 1387–1390.

Dragoş Alexandru Cojocaru and Ştefan Trăuşan Matu. 2015. Text generation starting from an ontology. In *Proceedings of the Romanian National Human-Computer Interaction Conference - RoCHI*, pages 55–60.

C. Maria Keet and Langa Khumalo. 2016. Toward a knowledge-to-text controlled natural language of isizulu. *Language Resources and Evaluation*, pages 1–27.

John P. McCrae, Penny Labropoulou, Jorge Gracia, Marta Villegas, Víctor Rodríguez-Doncel, and Philipp Cimiano, 2015. *ESWC (Satellite Events)*, chapter One Ontology to Bind Them All: The META-SHARE OWL Ontology for the Interoperability of Linguistic Datasets on the Web, pages 271–282.

Ehud Reiter and Robert Dale. 2000. *Building Natural Language Generation Systems*. Cambridge University Press.

Kamenka Staykova. 2014. Natural language generation and semantic technologies. *Cybernetics and Information Technologies*, 14(2):3–23.

Xiantang SUN and Chris MELLISH. 2006. Domain independent sentence generation from rdf representations for the semantic web. In *Combined Workshop on Language-Enabled Educational Technology and Development and Evaluation of Robust Spoken Dialogue Systems, European Conference on AI*.

Sandra Williams, Allan Third, and Richard Power. 2011. Levels of organisation in ontology verbalisation. In *13th European Workshop on Natural Language Generation*, pages 158–163. Proceedings of the 13th ENLG.

Comparing the template-based approach to GF: the case of Afrikaans

Lauren Sanby
Computer Science Dept.
University of Cape Town
Cape Town, South Africa

Ion Todd
Computer Science Dept.
University of Cape Town
Cape Town, South Africa

C. Maria Keet
Computer Science Dept.
University of Cape Town
Cape Town, South Africa

`{lauren.sanby,ion.todd}@alumni.uct.ac.za`   `mkeet@cs.uct.ac.za`

Abstract

Ontologies are usually represented in OWL that is not easy to grasp by domain experts. A solution to bridge this gap is to use a controlled natural language or natural language generation (NLG), which allows the knowledge in the ontology to be rendered automatically into a natural language. Several approaches exist to realise this. We used both templates and the Grammatical Framework (GF) and examined the feasibility of each by developing NLG modules for a language that had none: Afrikaans. The template system requires manual translation of the ontology's vocabulary into Afrikaans, if not already done so, while the GF system can translate the terms automatically. Yet, the template system is found to produce more grammatically correct sentences and verbalises the ontology slightly faster than the GF system. The template-based approach seems easier to extend for future development.

1   Introduction

The knowledge acquisition bottleneck is well known for many years, and many proposals have been made to ameliorate this problem. One such avenue is to avail of a natural language interface. This has gained traction in the Semantic Web community in the past 10 years; two recent surveys on this intersection serve to illustrate its relevance (Bouayad-Agha et al., 2014; Safwat and Davis, 2016). While a template-based approach to generate natural language from OWL files is popular (e.g., (Androutsopoulos et al., 2013; Third et al., 2011)), other approaches have been proposed, from 'patterns' (Keet and Khumalo, 2014) to specific grammars for controlled natural languages (Kuhn, 2013) to the comprehensive Grammatical Framework (GF) that principally serves to translate between natural languages (Gruzitis et al., 2010; Ranta, 2011). It is not clear what would be the 'best' approach and technology to generate sentences from OWL files, if any, which may depend more on the system requirements or on the grammar of the language. To this end, we used a fairly controlled experiment in building two NLG modules that take OWL files as input for a language that had none—Afrikaans—by two people with the similar background in computer science in the same time frame. The template-based approach included a formal specification of correctness of encoding and a proof-of concept implementation. The GF-based approach used GF and required substantial software development. Both were evaluated and compared.

The tools, source code, template specification and GF file, test data, output files, and further information on design, proofs, and analyses of the experiments are online at: `http://pubs.cs.uct.ac.za/honsproj/cgi-bin/view/2015/sanby_todd.zip/`.

2   Design of the verbalisers

The template-based approach followed an NLG system-oriented development process (Reiter, 1997), focussing on: surface realisation as to what should go in the templates, a formal proof of correctness of the templates with respect to OWL, and subsequent implementation. Surface realisation included design choices; e.g., 'must be' vs. 'at least one', which is illustrated here for 'is part of' in $Tak \sqsubseteq \exists is\_deel\_van.Boom$:

(1)   Elke tak moet <u>deel van</u> 'n boom <u>wees</u>
      'each branch must <u>be</u> <u>part of a tree</u>'

(2)   Elke tak <u>is deel van</u> ten minste een boom
      'each branch <u>is part of</u> at least one tree'

noting that the second option is easier in a template-based approach, because then the name of the OWL object property can be used directly in the template rather than requiring additional string and verb processing.

GF is a functional programming language that has an abstract grammar as an intermediate language and a concrete grammar that defines how components should be put together in a sentence (Ranta, 2011). The latter is language-dependent and thus needs to be changed when adding a new language (e.g., (Angelov and Ranta, 2009)). GF has an Afrikaans library, but it needed to be extended so as to create the specific grammar files needed for verbalising OWL 2 DL ontologies in Afrikaans. The GF system also required software development for GF↔OWL file interaction, resulting in the architecture depicted in Fig. 1.

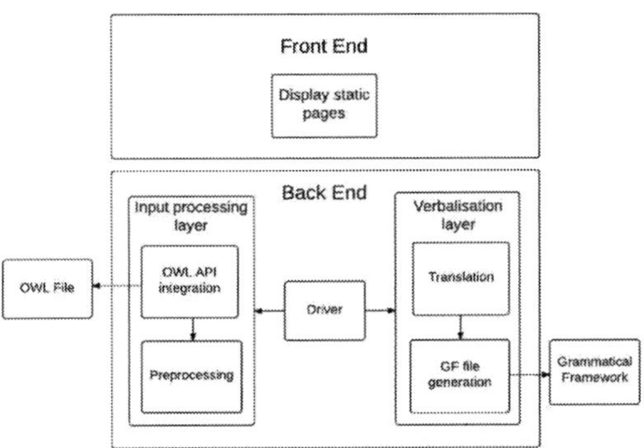

Figure 1: Architecture diagram for the GF approach. Preprocessing focuses on 'normalising' names from different ontologies, such as the property names *is-part-of* and *isPartOf*.

Let us illustrate the comparison of the declarative components with OWL's disjoint classes axiom. The template is specified in XML as follows:

```
<Constraint type="Disjoint">
    <Text>'n</Text>
        <Object index="0"/>
    <Text>is nie 'n</Text>
        <Object index="1"/>
    <Text>nie</Text>
</Constraint>
```

and the corresponding GF concrete grammar as:

```
DisjointClasses x y =
    {s="'n "++x.s++"is nie 'n"
        ++y.s++"nie"};
```

Then, with the first `Object index`, or `x`, being, say, *Dier* 'animal' and the second one (`y`) *Plant* 'plant', then the sentence 'n dier is nie 'n plant nie 'an animal is not a plant' is generated. These tem-

plates and GF concrete grammar have been specified for most OWL 2 DL language features (see online material).

3 Verbalisations compared

Six ontologies were verbalised in Afrikaans. Due to space limitations, we only include here a selection of a range of types of axioms to illustrate the output and compare the two; the observations hold equally for the other axioms of the same type and across ontologies. The wine ontology is used, as that is an important subject domain in the Western Cape where Afrikaans is spoken widely.

Taxonomic subsumption of named classes for, e.g., $Chianti \sqsubseteq ItalianWine$ 'Chianti is an italian wine' is verbalised as:

T: `Elke Chianti is 'n ItalianWyn.`

G: `elke [Chianti] is [ItalianWyn]`

where G (GF-based) misses the indeterminate article 'n that T (template-based) correctly has. Equivalent classes for 'Sweet wine is wine and has sugar with value sweet' are verbalised as:

T: `Elke SoetWyn (is Wyn en het suiker`
    `ten minste een Soet)`

G: `'n [SoetWyn] is [Wyn] en [HetSuiker]`
    `[Soet]`

The ontology is ambiguous in this regard due to the use of "value", and therewith making it unclear whether *ten minste een* 'at least one' is the the best. A class expression with a disjunction or a one-of construct uses *of* 'or' in both cases, illustrated here with a one-of in $Zinfandel \sqsubseteq \forall hasFlavor.\{Strong, Moderate\}$ 'Each Zinfandel has flavour only strong or moderate':

T: `Elke Zinfandel het net geur Gematig`
    `of Sterk`

G: `elke [Zinfandel] is iets wat`
    `[Gematig] of [Sterk] [HetGeur]`

noting that T's *net* 'only' is more precise with respect to the universal quantification in the axiom it verbalises and G's `het Geur` 'has flavour' is in the wrong place. Disjointness is correct in both cases, as in, e.g., $LateHarvest \sqsubseteq \neg EarlyHarvest$ 'Late harvest is not an early harvest':

T: `'n Laatoes is nie 'n VroeeOes nie.`

G: `'n [Laatoes] is nie 'n [VroeeOes]`
    `nie`

Object property range has valid alternatives; e.g., 'has sugar has as range wine sugar':

T: `Iets het net suiker WynSuiker`

G: `Elke ding wat is [HetSuiker] , is`
   `[WynSuiker]`

Inverse object properties also has two valid alternatives, although T is easier to read thanks to the shorthand *teenoorgestelde* 'opposite/inverse', as in, e.g., 'made from grape is inverse of made into wine':

T: `"gemaak in wyn" is die`
   `teenoorgestelde van "is gemaak van`
   `druiwe" (As X gemaak in wyn Y; Y is`
   `gemaak van druiwe X.).`

G: `As X [GemaakInWyn] Y dan Y`
   `[IsGemaakVanDruiwe] X. As X`
   `[IsGemaakVanDruiwe] Y dan Y`
   `[GemaakInWyn] X.`

The verbalisation of a functional property is correct and understandable, respectively, although they ignores whether a domain was declared, which was 'wine' in 'Each thing has color at most one wine color':

T: `Elke objek kan net een kleur hê.`

G: `Elke ding het een [HetKleur]`

The templates cover object property characteristics better; e.g., with *oorganklike* 'transitive' in T, where G misses the implication, and G does not have a verbalisation for symmetric.

ABox assertions are correct in both approaches as well, although the template-based one is again more readable also for different individuals, like in 'OffDry, dry, and sweet are all different', for *almal* 'all [of them]' fits with a sequence of more than two items compared:

T: `AfDroe en Droe en Soet is almal`
   `verskillend.`

G: `[AfDroe] , [Droe] en [Soet] is al`
   `verskillende`

The verbalisation of object subproperty was incorrect in both cases. G verbalised it as symmetric, whereas T stringed the two verbalised parts of the axiom together in the wrong order. Notwithstanding, we include it here, because it demonstrates that referring expressions were incorporated correctly, indicated with *dit* 'it':

T: `As iets het wyn descriptor, dit het`
   `suiker.`

(which ought to have read 'if something has sugar then it has a wine descriptor'). Data properties were not included in the GF-based approach, but were in the template-based approach, which contributes to the difference in number of axioms verbalised (see Table 1). As the template-based approach took less time to develop, this freed up time to make the sentence more natural language-like, such as addressing the capitalisation and changing the object property names from, e.g., `IsGemaakVanDruiwe` 'madeFromGrape' (as in the wine ontology) to `is gemaak van druiwe`.

4 Evaluation

We conducted two experiments with the proof-of-concept software to compare the two approaches.

4.1 Experiment set-up

The template and GF-based programs were tested using six OWL ontologies. Measures such a number of axioms verbalised and time taken were collected. In addition, a general comprehensibility of the verbalisation evaluation was conducted with a human domain expert who is an Afrikaans mother tongue speaker. The six sets of sentences were assigned a quality category on a 5-point Likert scale: 1. Incomprehensible; 2. Almost completely incomprehensible; 3. Somewhat understandable; 4. Understandable but obvious errors; 5. Easy to understand no obvious errors.

4.2 Results and Discussion

Table 1 includes the main quantitative results. Although the template program does not have 100% coverage for any of the ontologies, the only missing axioms are those that are explicitly ignored (data types, keys, universal class and property). The "sentences written" column shows that there is a difference in number of sentences generated for all the ontologies for that reason, whose detailed analysis is included in the online supplementary material.

The evaluation of the sentence quality is shown in Table 2. The quality of the template-based approach is higher on average, though not statistically significantly (Mann-Whitney, p=0.12852). This is mainly because more time was available to refine the templates than GF's concrete grammar.

As can be seen in Table 1, the template-based approach outperformed the GF-based approach on almost all measured metrics. It should be noted, however, that the GF-based approach includes also a translation module and generates the GF files dynamically. Also the GF↔OWL file interaction took extra time to develop, taking away time to refine the GF-based verbalisations. The on-the-fly translation takes more time to compute the results

Ontologies	|ax.|	Ax. verb.		Pct. verb.		Sent. written		Time (s)		Time/sent. (ms)	
		T	G	T	G	T	G	T	G	T	G
Pizza	712	707	711	99.3	99.9	707	711	1.7	2.1	2.4	3.0
African Wildlife	56	55	56	98.2	100.0	57	57	1.3	1.7	23.2	30.9
Computer Science	52	48	44	92.3	84.6	48	44	1.1	1.7	23.1	38.4
Wine	657	635	628	96.7	95.6	635	628	5.6	5.5	8.8	8.7
University	95	91	94	95.8	99.0	91	94	1.1	1.4	12.0	15.2
Stuff	136	134	110	98.5	80.9	175	110	1.2	1.5	6.9	13.7
Average				*96.8*	*93.3*	*285.5*	*273.8*	*2.0*	*2.3*	*12.7*	*18.3*

Table 1: Percentage ontology verbalisation for templates (T) and the GF program (G); |ax.| = total number of axioms; ax. verb. = axioms verbalised, pct. verb. = percentage verbalised; sent. = sentences.

Ontology	Template	GF
African Wildlife	5	4
Computer Science	4	4
Pizza	5	3
Stuff	4	2
University	4	4
Wine	4	4
Average	*4.4*	*3.5*

Table 2: Qualitative evaluation for the Grammar-based and template-based approaches.

compared to matching the OWL file with the templates in the XML file. While this is relatively minor with a small ontology, for a user to wait 6 seconds even with the wine ontology might become prohibitively slow with larger ontologies as well as in use cases that require runtime sentence generation. Finally, what also contributed to the template's success is Afrikaans, which has very few morphological issues and not a complex system of concordial agreement like, e.g., isiZulu (Keet and Khumalo, 2014), that is also spoken in South Africa.

5   Conclusions

There is no clear 'winner' between a template-based approach and GF when one has to start from scratch with a natural language that is relatively amenable to templates, such as Afrikaans. Both are feasible, with the GF-based approach requiring more upfront investment and the template-based approach being easier to understand and therefore easier to refine and extend, provided a multilingual system does not become a requirement.

References

I. Androutsopoulos, G. Lampouras, and D. Galanis. 2013. Generating natural language descriptions from owl ontologies: the naturalowl system. *Journal of Artificial Intelligence Research*, 48:671–715.

K. Angelov and A. Ranta. 2009. Implementing controlled languages in GF. In *Proc. of CNL'09*.

N. Bouayad-Agha, G. Casamayor, and L. Wanner. 2014. Natural language generation in the context of the semantic web. *Semantic Web J.*, 5(6):493–513.

N. Gruzitis, G. Nespore, and B. Saulite. 2010. Verbalizing ontologies in controlled baltic languages. In *Proc. of HLT–The Baltic Perspective*, volume 219 of *FAIA*, pages 187–194. IOS Press. Riga, Latvia.

C. M. Keet and L. Khumalo. 2014. Basics for a grammar engine to verbalize logical theories in isiZulu. In *Proc. of RuleML'14*, volume 8620 of *LNCS*, pages 216–225. Springer. Aug. 18-20, 2014, Prague, Czech Republic.

T. Kuhn. 2013. A principled approach to grammars for controlled natural languages and predictive editors. *J. of Logic, Lang. and Inf.*, 22(1):33–70.

A. Ranta. 2011. *Grammatical Framework: Programming with Multilingual Grammars*. CSLI Publications, Stanford.

R. Reiter, E. & Dale. 1997. Building applied natural language generation systems. *Natural Language Engineering*, 3:57–87.

H. Safwat and B. Davis. 2016. CNLs for the semantic web: a state of the art. *Language Resources & Evaluation*, in print:DOI: 10.1007/s10579–016–9351–x.

A. Third, S. Williams, and R. Power. 2011. OWL to English: a tool for generating organised easily-navigated hypertexts from ontologies. poster/demo paper, Open Unversity UK. ISWC'11, 23-27 Oct 2011, Bonn, Germany.

Generating Paraphrases from DBPedia using Deep Learning

Amin Sleimi
Université de Lorraine, Nancy (France)
`amin.sleimi@gmail.com`

Claire Gardent
CNRS/LORIA, Nancy (France)
`claire.gardent@loria.fr`

Abstract

Recent deep learning approaches to Natural Language Generation mostly rely on sequence-to-sequence models. In these approaches, the input is treated as a sequence whereas in most cases, input to generation usually is either a tree or a graph. In this paper, we describe an experiment showing how enriching a sequential input with structural information improves results and help support the generation of paraphrases.

1 Introduction

Following work by (Karpathy and Fei-Fei, 2015; Kiros et al., 2014; Vinyals et al., 2015; Fang et al., 2015; Xu et al., 2015; Devlin et al., 2014; Sutskever et al., 2011; Bahdanau et al., 2014; Luong et al., 2014), there has been much work recently on using deep learning techniques to generate text from data. (Wen et al., 2015) uses recurrent neural network to generate text from dialog speech acts. Using biography articles and infoboxes from the WikiProject Biography, (Lebret et al., 2016) learns a conditional neural language model to generate text from infoboxes. etc.

A basic feature of these approaches is that both the input and the output data is represented as a *sequence* so that generation can then be modeled using a Long Short Term Memory Model (LSTM) or a conditional language model.

Mostly however, the data taken as input by natural language generation systems is *tree or graph structured*, not linear.

In this paper, we investigate a constrained generation approach where the input is enriched with constraints on the syntactic shape of the sentence to be generated. As illustrated in Figure 1, there is a strong correlation between the shape

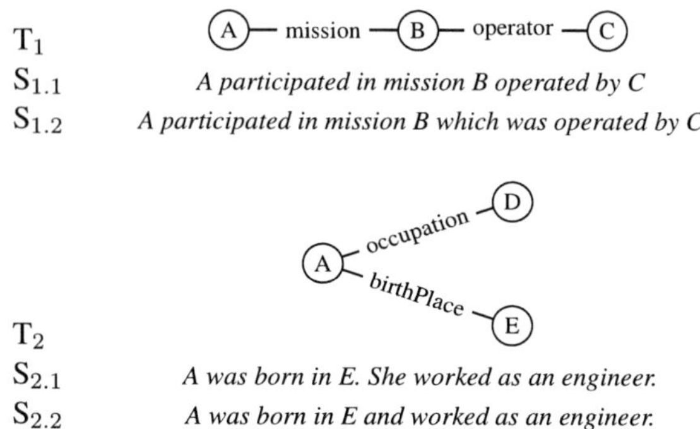

Figure 1: Input and Output Shapes (A = Susan Helms, B = STS 78, C = NASA, D = engineer, E = Charlotte, North Carolina).

of the input and the shape of the corresponding sentence. The chaining structure T_1 where B is shared by two predications (mission and operator) will favour the use of a participial or a passive subject relative clause. In contrast, the tree structure T_2 will favour the use of a new clause with pronominal subject or a coordinated VP. Using synthetic data, we explore different ways of integrating structural constraints in the training data. We focus on the following two questions.

1. Does structural information improve performance ?

We compare an approach where the structure of the input and of the corresponding paraphrase is made explicit in the training data with one where it is left implicit. We show that a model trained on a corpus making this information explicit helps improve the quality of the generated sentences.

2. Can structural information be used to generate paraphrases ?

Our experiments indicates that training on corpora making explicit structural information in the input data permits generating not one but several sentences from the same input.

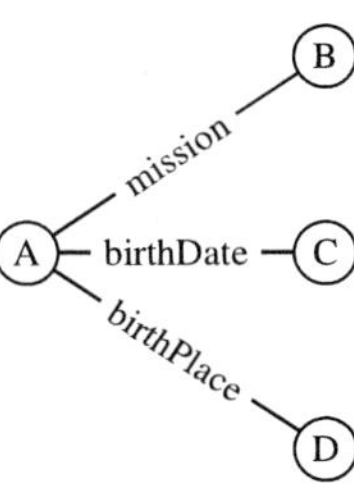

Figure 2: Example Input Graph (Subject and Object names have been replaced by capital letters)

In this first case study, we restrict ourselves to input data of the form illustrated in Figure 2 (i.e., input data consisting of three DBPedia triples related by a shared subject $(e\ p1\ e1)\ (e\ p2\ e2)\ (e\ p3\ e3))$ and explore different strategies for learning to generate paraphrases using the sequence-to-sequence model described in (Sutskever et al., 2011).

2 Training Corpus

To learn our sequence-to-sequence models for generation and to test our hypotheses, we build a synthetic training data-to-text corpus for generation which consists of 18 397 (data,text) pairs split into 11039 pairs for training, 7358 for development and 7358 for testing.

We build this corpus by extracting data from DBPEdia using SPARQL queries and by generating text using an existing surface realiser. As a result, each training item associates a given input shape (the shape of the RDF tree from DBPedia) with several output shapes (the syntactic shapes of the sentences generated from the RDF data by our surface realiser). Figure 3 shows an example input data and the corresponding paraphrases.

2.1 Data

RDF triples consist of (subject property object) tuples such as (Alan Bean occupation Test pilot). As illustrated in Figure 1, RDF data can be represented by a graph in which edges are labelled with properties and vertices with subject and object resources.

To construct a corpus of RDF data units which can serve as input for NLG, we retrieve sets of RDF triples from DBPedia SPARQL endpoint.

Given a DBPedia category (e.g., Astronaut), we define a SPARQL query that searches for all entities of this category which have a given set of properties. The query then returns all sets of RDF triples which satisfy this query. For instance, for the category Astronaut , we use the SPARQL query shown in Figure 4. Using this query, we extract sets of DBPedia triples corresponding to 634 entities (astronauts).

2.2 Text

To associate data with text, we build lexical entries for DBPedia properties and use a small handwritten grammar to automatically generate text from sets of DBPedia triples using the GenI generator (Gardent and Kow, 2007).

Lexicon. The lexicon is constructed semi-automatically by tokenizing the RDF triples and creating a lexical entry for each RDF resource. Subject and Object RDF resources trigger the automatic creation of a noun phrase where the string is simply the name of the corresponding resource (e.g., *John E Blaha, San Antonio, ...*). For properties, we manually create verb entries and assign each property a given lexicalisation. For instance, the property birthDate is mapped to the lexicalisation *was born on*.

Grammar. We use a simple Feature-Based Lexicalised Tree Adjoining Grammar which captures canonical clauses (1a), subject relative clauses (1b), VP coordination (1c) and sentence coordination (1d). Given this grammar, the lexicon described in the previous section and the RDF triple shown in (1a), the GenI generator generates the five verbalisations shown in five (1b-f).

(1) a. *John E Blaha was born on 1942 08 26*

   b. *John E Blaha who was born in San Antonio worked as a fighter pilot*

   c. *John E Blaha was born on 1942 08 26 and worked as a fighter pilot.*

   d. *John E Blaha was born on 1942 08 26. He is from United States*

   e. *John E Blaha was born on 1942 08 26 . He was born in San Antonio and worked as a fighter pilot*

Input	(JohnBlaha birthDate 1942_08_26) (JohnBlaha birthPlace SanAntonio) (JohnBlaha occupation Fighterpilot)
Simpl.Input	JohnBlaha birthDate 1942_08_26 birthPlace SanAntonio occupation Fighterpilot
S1	*John Blaha who was born on 1942 08 26 was born in San Antonio. He worked as Fighter pilot*
S2	*John Blaha was born on 1942 08 26 and worked as Fighter pilot. He was born in San Antonio*
S3	*John Blaha was born on 1942 08 26 and was born in San Antonio. He is from United States*
S4	*John Blaha was born on 1942 08 26. He was born in San Antonio and worked as Fighter pilot*
S5	*John Blaha was born on 1942 08 26 . He is from United States and was born in San Antonio*
C-Input	JohnBlaha (birthDate 1942_08_26) birthPlace SanAntonio . occupation Fighterpilot

Figure 3: Example Data, Associated Paraphrases and Constrained Input from the Training Corpus

```
1   [
2   PREFIX rdfs: <http://www.w3.org/2000/01/rdf-schema#>
3   PREFIX rdf: <http://www.w3.org/1999/02/22-rdf-syntax-ns#>
4   PREFIX foaf: <http://xmlns.com/foaf/0.1/>
5   PREFIX dbo: <http://dbpedia.org/ontology/>
6
7   SELECT ?x ?birthDate (SAMPLE(?bP) as ?birthPlace)
8   ?deathDate (SAMPLE(?dP) as ?deathPlace) ?occupation
9   ?status ?nationality ?mission
10                  WHERE {
11
12            ?x rdf:type <http://dbpedia.org/ontology/Astronaut> .
13            OPTIONAL {?x dbpedia2:birthPlace ?bP . }
14            OPTIONAL {?x dbpedia2:birthDate ?birthDate .}
15            OPTIONAL {?x dbpedia2:deathPlace ?dP .}
16            OPTIONAL {?x dbpedia2:deathDate ?deathDate .}
17       OPTIONAL {?x dbpedia2:occupation ?occupation .}
18       OPTIONAL {?x dbpedia2:status ?status .}
19       OPTIONAL {?x dbpedia2:nationality ?nationality .}
20       OPTIONAL {?x dbpedia2:mission ?mission .}
21
22                  }
23   ]
```

Figure 4: The sparql query to DBPedia endpoint for the Astronaut corpus

3 Learning

To learn a sequence-to-sequence model that can generate sentences from RDF data, we use the neural model described in (Sutskever et al., 2011) and the code distributed by Google Inc[1].

We experiment with different versions of the training corpus.

Raw corpus (BL). This is our a baseline system. In this case, the model is trained on the corpus of (data,text) pairs as is. No explicit information about the structure of the output is added to the data.

Raw Corpus+Structure Identifier (R+I). Each input data is associated with a structure identifier corresponding to one of the five syntactic shapes shown in Figure 3.

Raw corpus+Infix Connectors (R+C). The input data is enriched with infix connectors where & specifies conjunction, parentheses indicate a relative clause and "." sentence segmentation. The last line in Figure 3 shows the R+C input for S1.

4 Evaluation and Results.

We evaluate the results by computing the BLEU-4 score of the generated sentences against the reference sentence. Table 1 shows the results.

The baseline and the R+I model have very low results. For the baseline model, this indicates that training on a corpus where the same input is associated with several distinct paraphrases make it difficult to learn a good data-to-text generation model.

The marked difference between the R+I and the RI+C model shows that simply associating each input with an identifier labelling the syntactic structure of the associated sentence is not sufficient to learn a model that should predict different syntactic structures for differently labelled inputs. Interestingly, training on a corpus where the input data is enriched with infixed connectors giving indications about the structure of the associated sentence yields much better results.

5 Conclusion

Using synthetic data, we presented an experiment which suggests that enriching the data input to

---

[1]https://github.com/tensorflow/
tensorflow/tree/master/tensorflow/
models/rnn/translate

System	S1	S2	S3	S4	S5
BL	3.6	5.9	6.6	5.9	7.5
R+I	4.0	6.5	6.9	6.5	8.2
R+C	98.2	91.7	91.6	88.8	89.1

Table 1: BLEU-4 scores

generation with information about the corresponding sentence structure (i) helps improve performance and (ii) permits generating paraphrases.

Further work involves three main directions.

First, the results obtained in this first case study should be tested for genericity . That is the synthetic data approach we presented here should be tested on a larger scale taking into account input structures of different types (chaining vs branching) and different sizes.

Second, the approach should be extended and tested on "real data" i.e., on a training corpus where the DBPEdia triples used as input data are associated with sentences produced by humans and where there is consequently, no direct information about their structure.

Third, we plan to investigate how various deep learning techniques, in particular, recursive neural networks, could be used to capture the correlation between input data and sentence structure.

Acknowledgments

We thank the French National Research Agency for funding the research presented in this paper in the context of the WebNLG project ANR-14-CE24-0033.

References

Dzmitry Bahdanau, Kyunghyun Cho, and Yoshua Bengio. 2014. Neural machine translation by jointly learning to align and translate. *arXiv preprint arXiv:1409.0473.*

Jacob Devlin, Rabih Zbib, Zhongqiang Huang, Thomas Lamar, Richard M Schwartz, and John Makhoul. 2014. Fast and robust neural network joint models for statistical machine translation. In *ACL (1)*, pages 1370–1380. Citeseer.

Hao Fang, Saurabh Gupta, Forrest Iandola, Rupesh K Srivastava, Li Deng, Piotr Dollár, Jianfeng Gao, Xiaodong He, Margaret Mitchell, John C Platt, et al. 2015. From captions to visual concepts and back. In *Proceedings of the IEEE Conference on Computer Vision and Pattern Recognition*, pages 1473–1482.

C. Gardent and E. Kow. 2007. A symbolic approach to near-deterministic surface realisation using tree adjoining grammar. In *ACL07*.

Andrej Karpathy and Li Fei-Fei. 2015. Deep visual-semantic alignments for generating image descriptions. In *Proceedings of the IEEE Conference on Computer Vision and Pattern Recognition*, pages 3128–3137.

Ryan Kiros, Ruslan Salakhutdinov, and Richard S Zemel. 2014. Unifying visual-semantic embeddings with multimodal neural language models. *arXiv preprint arXiv:1411.2539*.

R. Lebret, D. Grangier, and M. Auli. 2016. Generating Text from Structured Data with Application to the Biography Domain. *ArXiv e-prints*, March.

Minh-Thang Luong, Ilya Sutskever, Quoc V Le, Oriol Vinyals, and Wojciech Zaremba. 2014. Addressing the rare word problem in neural machine translation. *arXiv preprint arXiv:1410.8206*.

Ilya Sutskever, James Martens, and Geoffrey E Hinton. 2011. Generating text with recurrent neural networks. In *Proceedings of the 28th International Conference on Machine Learning (ICML-11)*, pages 1017–1024.

Oriol Vinyals, Alexander Toshev, Samy Bengio, and Dumitru Erhan. 2015. Show and tell: A neural image caption generator. In *Proceedings of the IEEE Conference on Computer Vision and Pattern Recognition*, pages 3156–3164.

Tsung-Hsien Wen, Milica Gasic, Nikola Mrksic, Pei-Hao Su, David Vandyke, and Steve Young. 2015. Semantically conditioned ltsm-base natural language generation for spoken dialogue systems. In *Proceedings of the 2015 Conference on Empirical Methods in Computational Linguistics*, pages 1711–1721.

Kelvin Xu, Jimmy Ba, Ryan Kiros, Aaron Courville, Ruslan Salakhutdinov, Richard Zemel, and Yoshua Bengio. 2015. Show, attend and tell: Neural image caption generation with visual attention. *arXiv preprint arXiv:1502.03044*.

Automatic Tweet Generation From Traffic Incident Data

Khoa Tran
School of Computing Science
Simon Fraser University
Burnaby, BC, CANADA
khoa_tran@sfu.ca

Fred Popowich
School of Computing Science
Simon Fraser University
Burnaby, BC, CANADA
popowich@sfu.ca

Abstract

We examine the use of traffic information with other knowledge sources to automatically generate natural language tweets similar to those created by humans. We consider how different forms of information can be combined to provide tweets customized to a particular location and/or specific user. Our approach is based on data-driven natural language generation (NLG) techniques using corpora containing examples of natural language tweets. It specifically draws upon semantic data and knowledge developed and used in the web based Connected Vehicles and Smart Transportation system. We introduce an alignment model, generation model and location-based user model which will together support location-relevant information delivery. We provide examples of our system output and discuss evaluation issues with generated tweets.

1 Introduction

Traffic congestion continues to be a major problem in large cities around the world, and a source of frustration for commuters, commercial drivers, tourists, and even occasional drivers. Current efforts to reduce congestion and frustration often involve providing road users with real-time traffic information to help estimate travel time accurately, resulting in better route planning and travel decisions (Tseng et al., 2013). The different approaches to deliver traffic information include radio, smart navigation devices and social networks.

Information from radio and social networks is delivered as messages, which consist primarily of natural language. When delivered on smart navigation devices, information is presented with colour and icons on interactive maps; for example, congested road segments are usually in red while clear road segments are in green [1].

Text and audio messages associated with radio and social network channels are mainly human-generated, requiring time and effort. The information sources for these messages primarily uses the same data used as smart navigation devices in conjunction with camera images, eye-witness reports and other sources, which collectively require substantial effort and time. Although several social network channels may use computer programs (i.e., "bots") to generate messages automatically from a data source, these messages are constructed using strict templates which appear to users as cold, unnatural, distant and unreliable.

2 Our Approach

We look at the role of natural language generation (NLG) in the context of a system that automatically generate messages about traffic incidents. Our approach is based on data-driven NLG techniques where corpora containing examples of natural language tweets are used to train the model to generate natural language texts. It draws upon semantic data and knowledge developed and used in the web based Connected Vehicles and Smart Transportation (CVST) system (Tizghadam and Leon-Garcia, 2015). We introduce an alignment model, generation model and location-based user model which together support location-relevant information delivery.

We design a traffic notification system having a location-based user model to predict a user's routes and deliver real-time notifications if traffic incidents occur. Figure 1 shows the design of our proposed system. The GPS location of a user is

---

[1] Google Maps uses this colour code as described in https://support.google.com/maps/answer/3092439?hl=en&rd=1

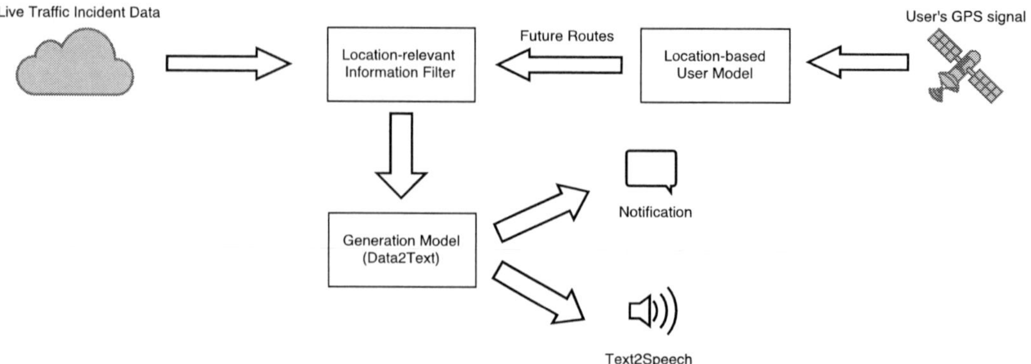

Figure 1: The traffic notification system that notifies location-relevant traffic information for road users.

processed through the location-based user model. It predicts a ranked list of routes and destinations the user could take. Concurrently, a live stream of traffic incidents is collected and forwarded to the location-relevant information filter. This component applies a location filter on the traffic incident data based on the predicted user's routes and destinations. The output is the data scenarios of traffic incidents that happen on or nearby the routes the user may take. Next, the generation model composes short messages describing nearby traffic incidents. These messages are sent to users as textual or speech notifications using a text-to-speech system.

We construct our corpus from two data-sets from the CVST APIs [2]. The first data-set is a collection of 13,667 tweets mentioning traffic incidents in the greater Toronto area of Canada. The second data-set consists of 27,795 records concerning road incidents in greater Toronto. Using incident times and locations from the two data-sets, we are able to match tweets with the road incidents to construct a corpus of road incidents with their corresponding tweets. We also explore other traffic related data-sets that can be used to train our system. However, using such data is restricted as discussed in Section 4.1. On the other hand, for each road incident in our constructed corpus, we are able to collect more than one tweet from different users mentioning the event. Utilizing these human-generated texts ensures better output quality for our NLG system.

Using the constructed corpus, we apply an existing semantic alignment model (Section 4.2) to learn the semantic correspondences between data

records and their textual descriptions in the tweets. Then, we apply a model for concept-to-text generation (Section 4.3) to generate tweets about traffic incidents from given records. However, our system's output is not limited to tweet generation. Output can be personalized, for example, as a virtual assistant, to generate traffic notifications for users based on their driving routines incorporating daily routes, departure and arrival times, and specific locations. Previous work on capturing users' locations and route prediction (Section 4.4) can be applied to select only the potentially user-interested traffic information and deliver it to the drivers.

The evaluation of automatically generated tweets can be approached from several perspectives. Evaluation in the context of the task outlined in Figure 1 can involve human subjects, looking at metrics such as the usefulness of tweets (using rating criteria like those in rating the helpfulness of reviews or comments), and the quality of tweets (involving fluency and readability). Detailed human evaluation of the tweets is beyond the scope of the current research. Our plan is to focus on automated techniques in the evaluation of the automatically generated tweets, given that we have a gold-standard of human generated data. To evaluate our models, we build on previous evaluation techniques such as BLEU and METEOR (Konstas, 2014).

3 Related work

Recent work in automatic tweet generation focuses on the tasks of automatic text summarization and topic classification. Lloret and Palomar (2013) present a framework that automatically

<hr>

[2]http://portal.cvst.ca

generates twitter headlines for journal articles using text summarization approaches. Analogously, by applying different text processing techniques including content grouping, topic classification and text summarization, Lofi and Krestel (2012) develop a system that generates tweets from government documents. Krokos and Samet (2014) also utilize several sentiment analysis and classification methods in their approach to automatically discover and generate hashtags for tweets that do not have user-generated hashtags. On the other hand, Sidhaye and Cheung (2015) use different metrics and statistics to show that most tweets cannot be re-constructed from the original articles that they reference; concluding that applying extractive summarization methods to generate indicative tweets could be a limitation.

Our work focuses on another aspect where tweets are constructed from structured data, and in our case the data can come from a real-time web application. Our generation task is also known as data-to-text, concept-to-text or linguistic description of data generation. The domain of our NLG work is novel with respect to the previous work in different domains including weather forecasts (Ramos-Soto et al., 2015a), educational reports (Bontcheva and Wilks, 2004; Ramos-Soto et al., 2015b) and clinical reports (Portet et al., 2009).

Although the results from previous work are promising and some proven to be better than human-generated content, they still have limitations. Most current approaches are based on very specific rules or grammars. Therefore, adapting these systems to a different data-set or domain usually requires re-designing the entire system again. However, data-driven techniques are applicable to different domains (Liang et al., 2009; Angeli et al., 2010; Kim and Mooney, 2010; Konstas, 2014). These approaches define probabilistic models that can be trained to learn the patterns and hidden alignments between data and text, thereby avoiding the construction of rules and grammars that require domain-specific knowledge.

We focus on a generation system that can apply to different types of traffic data-sets (road closures, road incidents, traffic flow, etc.). We use an existing alignment model (Liang et al., 2009) to learn the semantic correspondences between traffic data and its textual description. Konstas (2014)'s concept-to-text generation approach is used for the automatic generation of tweets to be ultimately incorporated into a real-time system.

Overall, we chose our data-driven approach since it is location independent; different cities have different kinds of traffic data, information road closures, road incidents, road conditions each with different kinds of data structures. We can handle different data-sets without changing the model structure, incorporating it into an end-to-end system with surface realisation and content planning in one model.

4 The Task

A data entry $\mathbf{d}$ consists of a set of records $\mathbf{r} = \{r_1, r_2, ..., r_n\}$. Each record is described with a record type $r_i.t$, $1 \leq i \leq |\mathbf{r}|$, and a set of fields $\mathbf{f}$. Each field $f_j \in \mathbf{f}$, $1 \leq j \leq |\mathbf{f}|$, has a field type $f_j.t$ and a value $f_j.v$. A scenario in the training corpus is a pair of $(\mathbf{d}, \mathbf{w})$ where $\mathbf{w}$ is the text describing the data entry $\mathbf{d}$. Our goal is to train a model that represents the hidden alignments between data entry $\mathbf{d}$ and the observed text $\mathbf{w}$ in the training corpus. Then, the trained model that captures the alignment is used to generate text $\mathbf{g}$ from a new entry $\mathbf{d}$ not contained in the training corpus.

4.1 Dataset

There are various types of traffic-related data including traffic flow, traffic incidents, road constructions and road closures. Such data is usually available through different map and road navigation APIs such as Tom Tom Traffic[3], Google Maps[4] and Bing Maps[5] or government open data sources. Despite the wide availability of traffic-related data, most of the data are only useful for visualisation purposes since they lack the corresponding textual descriptions. A few of the data sources have a short description associated with each data entry such as Dublin City Council's road works and maintenance[6] and Bing Maps' Traffic Incidents[7]. However, the text description is not sufficiently detailed to cover essential information in the data entry.

The CVST project has APIs for different traffic-related data-sets of greater Toronto area including traffic cameras and sensors, road closures and in-

---

[3]http://developer.tomtom.com/
[4]https://developers.google.com/maps/
[5]https://www.bingmapsportal.com/
[6]https://data.dublinked.ie/dataset/roads-maintenance-annual-works-programme
[7]https://msdn.microsoft.com/en-us/library/hh441726.aspx

cidents, public transportation and tweets. We use two data-sets from the CVST APIs, road incidents and twitter incidents, to construct our corpus. The road incidents data-set has details about traffic incidents such as time, location, type and reason. The twitter incidents data-set contains basic information about the incident and its related tweets.

By matching times and locations of records in the two data-sets, we construct a parallel corpus of traffic incidents with their related tweets. However, the times and locations from the two datasets are not always exactly matched. Therefore, we allow errors when matching these values. We consider two incidents from two data-sets to be matched if:

- the events' locations are within 100 meters from each other,

- and the events' start times are within 90 minutes of each other

The data is collected from January 2015 to May 2016. There are 27,795 records in road incident data-set and 13,134 records with 13,667 tweets in the twitter incident data-set (some records have more than one associated tweets). After matching the two data-sets using the described rules, we have a corpus of 1,388 incidents and 2,829 tweets. The tweets are crawled from Twitter and are generated by both humans and machines.

4.2 The alignment model

Liang et al. (2009) introduce a hierarchical semi-Markov model to learn the correspondences between a world state and an unsegmented stream of text. Their approach is a generative process with three main components:

- Record choice: choose a sequence of records $r = (r_1, ..., r_{|\mathbf{r}|})$ where each $r_i \in \mathbf{d}$ and has a record type $r_i.t$. The choice of consecutive records depends on their types.

- Field choice: for each chosen record r_i, select a sequence of fields $\mathbf{f}_i = (f_{i1}, ..., f_{i|\mathbf{f}_i|})$ where each $f_{ij} \in \{1, ..., m\}$.

- Word choice: for each chosen field f_{ij}, choose a number $c_{ij} > 0$ and generate a sequence of c_{ij} words.

Their record choice model is described as a Markov chain of records conditioned on record types. Their intention is to capture salience and coherence. Formally:

$$p(\mathbf{r} \mid \mathbf{d}) = \prod_{i=1}^{|\mathbf{r}|} p(r_i.t \mid r_{i-1}.t) \frac{1}{\mid \mathbf{s}(r_i.t) \mid}$$

where $\mathbf{s}(r_i.t)$ is the set of records in $\mathbf{d}$ that has record type $r_i.t$ and $r_0.t$ is the START record type. Their model also includes a special NULL record type responsible for generating text that does not belong to any real record types. Analogously, field choice model is a Markov chain of fields conditioned on the choice of records:

$$p(\mathbf{f} \mid \mathbf{r}) = \prod_{i=1}^{|\mathbf{r}|} \prod_{j=1}^{|\mathbf{f}_j|} p(f_{ij} \mid f_{i(j-1)})$$

Two special fields — START and STOP — are also implemented to capture the transitions at the boundaries of the phrases. In addition, each record type has a NULL field aligned to words that refer to that record type in general. The final step of the process is the word choice model where words are generated from the choice of records and fields. Specifically, for each field f_{ij}, we generate a number of words c_{ij}, chosen uniformly. Then the words $\mathbf{w}$ are generated conditioned on the field $\mathbf{f}$.

$$p(\mathbf{w} \mid \mathbf{r}, \mathbf{f}, \mathbf{c}, \mathbf{d}) = \prod_{k=1}^{|\mathbf{w}|} p_w(w_k \mid r(k).t_{f(k)}, r(k).v_{f(k)})$$

where $r(k)$ and $f(k)$ are record and field responsible for generating word w_k and $p_w(w_k \mid t, v)$ is the distribution of words given a field type t and field value v. Their model supports three different field types. Depending on the field types, Liang et al. 2009 define different methods for generating words:

- Integer type: generate the exact value, rounding up, rounding down and adding or subtracting unexplained noise ϵ_+ or ϵ_-

- String type: generate a word chosen uniformly from those in the field value

- Categorical type: maintain a separate multinomial distribution over words for each field value in the category.

G_{CS}	1. $S \rightarrow R(start)$	$[Pr = 1]$
	2. $R(r_i.t) \rightarrow FS(r_j, start)\, R(r_j.t)$	$\left[P(r_j.t \mid r_i.t)\frac{1}{|\mathbf{s}(r_j.t)|}\right]$
	3. $R(r_i.t) \rightarrow FS(r_j, start)$	$\left[P(r_j.t \mid r_i.t)\frac{1}{|\mathbf{s}(r_j.t)|}\right]$
	4. $FS(r, r.f_i) \rightarrow F(r, r.f_j)FS(r, r.f_j)$	$[P(f_j \mid f_i)]$
	5. $FS(r, r.f_i) \rightarrow F(r, r.f_j)$	$[P(f_j \mid f_i)]$
	6. $F(r, r.f) \rightarrow W(r, r.f)F(r, r.f)$	$[P(w \mid w_{-1}, r, r.f)]$
	7. $F(r, r.f) \rightarrow W(r, r.f)$	$[P(w \mid w_{-1}, r, r.f)]$
G_{SURF}	8. $W(r, r.f) \rightarrow \alpha$	$[P(\alpha \mid r, r.f, f.t, f.v, f.t = cat, null)]$
	9. $W(r, r.f) \rightarrow gen(f.v)$	$[P(gen(f.v).mode \mid r, r.f, f.t = int)\times$ $P(f.v \mid gen(f.v).mode)]$
	10. $W(r, r.f) \rightarrow gen\_str(f.v, i)$	$[Pr = 1]$

Table 1: Grammar rules used for generation with their corresponding weights.

4.3 The generation model

Konstas (2014) recasts an earlier model (Liang et al., 2009) into a set of context-free grammar (CFG) rules. To capture word-to-word dependencies during the generation process, he added more rules to emit a chain of words, rather than words in isolation. Table 1 shows his defined grammar rules with their corresponding weights.

The first rule in the grammar expands from a start symbol S to a special START record $R(start)$. Then, the chain of two consecutive records, r_i and r_j is defined through rule (2) and (3). Their weight is the probability of emitting record r_j given record r_i and corresponds to the record choice model of Liang et al. (2009). Equivalently, rule (4) and (5) define the chain of two consecutive fields, f_i followed by f_j, and their weight corresponds to the field choice model. Rule (6) and (7) are added to specify the expansion of field F to a sequence of words W. Their weight is the bigram probability of the current word given its previous word, the current record and field. Finally, rules (8)-(10) are responsible for generating words. If the field type is categorical (denoted as cat) or NULL (denoted as $null$), rule (8) is applied to generate a single word α in the vocabulary of the training set. Its weight is the probability of seeing α, given the current record, field and the field type is cat or $null$. Rule (9) is applied if the field type is integer (denoted as int). $gen(f.v)$ is a function that accepts the field value (an integer) as its input and return an integer using one of the six methods described by Liang et al. (2009). The weight is a multinomial distribution over the six integer generation function choices, given the record field f, times $P(f.v \mid gen(f.v).mode)]$, which is set to the geometric distribution of noise

ϵ_+ and ϵ_-, or to 1 otherwise (Konstas, 2014). Rule (10) is responsible for generating a word for string-type field. $gen\_str(f.v, i)$ is a function that simply return the ith word of the string in the field value $f.v$.

After defining the grammar rules, Konstas (2014) treats the generation problem as a parsing problem using the CFG rules. He uses a modified version of the CYK algorithm (Kasami, 1966; Younger, 1967) to find the best text $\mathbf{w}$ given a structured data entry $\mathbf{d}$. His basic decoder is presented as a deductive proof system (Shieber et al., 1995) in Table 2. The decoding process works in a bottom-up fashion. It starts with choosing N — the length (number of words) of the output text. Konstas (2014) determines N using a simple linear regression model where features being record-field pairs in the data entry $\mathbf{d}$. Then, for each position i in the output text, it searches for the best scoring item that spans from i to $i + 1$ (one single word). Next, items are visited and combined in order for larger spans until it reaches the goal item $[S, 0, N]$ — symbol S spans from position 0 to N.

The basic decoder always chooses the best scoring item during the parsing process. Konstas (2014) extends the basic decoder with the k-best decoder in which a list of k-best derivations will be kept for each item. The extension significantly improves the output quality by avoiding local optimums. He also intersects the grammar rules with a tri-gram language model and a dependency model to ensure fluency and grammaticality of the output text.

4.4 Location-based user model

There has been wide range of work on location-based user models, learning and predicting users' routes and destinations. These tasks involve some

Items:	$[A, i, j]$
	$R(A \rightarrow B)$
	$R(A \rightarrow BC)$
Axioms:	$[W, i, i+1] : s \qquad W \rightarrow g_{i+1}, g_{i+1} \in \{\alpha, \text{gen}(), \text{gen\_str}()\}$
Inference rules:	
(1)	$\dfrac{R(A \rightarrow B):s\,[B,i,j]:s_1}{[A,i,j]:s \cdot s_1}$
(2)	$\dfrac{R(A \rightarrow BC):s\,[B,i,k]:s_1\,[C,k,j]:s_2}{[A,i,j]:s \cdot s_1 \cdot s_2}$
Goal:	$[S, 0, N]$

Table 2: The basic decoder deductive system.

uncertainties. Much work relies on GPS signal data to identify a user's location and may not be accurate. In addition, intended destinations are not always certain since they may be affected by factors such as weather, traffic, day of week, and time of day. Due to many uncertainties arising from the task, most systems build probabilistic models to identify and predict users' locations. Marmasse and Schmandt (2000, 2002) apply pattern recognition techniques to learn users' patterns of traveling and frequent destinations. These frequent locations can be added or removed manually by users. Then, each location is assigned to a to-do list which is displayed whenever users travel to this location. In Krumm et al. (2013)'s model, the map can be modelled as a directed graph where road intersections are vertices and road segments connecting these intersections are edges. A probabilistic model is used to rank the potential destinations based on the current trip (previous intersections users have passed). After collecting a list of candidate destinations and their probabilities, route probabilities are computed by summing all destination probabilities along the fastest routes. Therefore, a corpus of the driver's regular routes is not necessary in this model. Simons et al. (2006) use a Hidden Markov Model (HMM) with the extended version where they consider factors such as day of week and time of travel in their prediction algorithms, while Liao et al. (2007) use a more complex HMM with the ability to infer the user's mode of transportation.

5   Examples

Table 3 presents an example of input and output of the generation model with different settings. In the first setting, we train the weights of the grammar rules using the whole corpus. Next, we use the k-best decoder integrated with a tri-gram language model to generate the text given the input scenario. We try different values of k (the number of k-best derivations kept for each item during the generation process). The generation system generates output 1a and output 1b for $k = 10$ and $k = 20$ respectively. We can try with larger values of k, however, it will affect the generation time, which becomes a factor if incorporated into a real time system. In the above example, instead of using the whole corpus, we use only tweets from a specific user to train the model. The chosen tweets in the second setting are generated by the user "680 NEWS Traffic" who has the majority of tweets in the corpus. We also try different k values ($k = 10$ and $k = 20$), however, the results are the same and presented in output 2.

Some essential records such as "Reference road" and "Reason" from the input scenario are not chosen by the generator for inclusion in the generated tweets in output 1a and output 2 respectively. On the other hand, extra information that the input does not cover is included arbitrarily such as "collision", "the right lane" or "the left lane". There are two main reasons for this behavior:

- inaccurate alignments between data and text: all the alignments are inferred from an unannotated corpus. A fully or partially annotated corpus will improve the accuracy of the alignment model.

- corpus: usually, the tweets contain more information than the structured data. This extra information can create noise in the training process, especially without supervision.

6   Conclusions and Future Work

The preliminary results for the data-driven approaches show that it is possible to generate real-time tweets for inclusion in a real-time traffic notification system, using techniques that are oth-

Input	Main road		Reference road	Lane	Stream
	Name	**Direction**	**Name**	**Value**	**Value**
	401	Eastbound	Yonge St	collectors	collectors
	Condition	**Reason**	**Incident type**		
	Value	**Value**	**Value**		
	Bad traffic	Disabled vehicle	Disabled vehicle		
Output 1a	collision: collision: #hwy401 eb express at yonge st				
Output 1b	401 collectors - right lane blocked with a collision.				
Output 2	eb 401 at yonge express, blocking the left lane				

Table 3: Example input and output of the generation system with different settings.

erwise applicable to different domains and data-sets. There are various types and sources of traffic-related data useful to drivers (e.g. traffic flow, road construction,...), and we have only scratched the surface of the issues concerning personalized tweets. Further evaluation is required and we will present the preliminary results from automatic evaluation during the workshop.

A high priority for the ongoing research is the content-preference model: some users desire certain information more than other information (e.g. reason of the accident, detour information, ...). A content-preference model can be integrated into the grammar to re-rank the generated sentences with the information users need.

Given the relatively constrained domain, we want to consider how template based models can be used with the data-driven approach introduced in this paper. A template approach requires different set of patterns and rules for each traffic data type, but integrating techniques involving semantic role labels (Lindberg et al., 2013) may assist in applying our approach to different data-sets and different locations.

Another aspect we need to consider to improve the system is how can we optimize it in terms of output quality and generation time. For output quality, considering the limitation described in section 5, we may want to get more data and potentially annotate parts of the data to get better alignment accuracy. In addition, applying different data pre-processing and normalizing techniques can also help clean up the data before training the model. To improve the generation time, we can apply an approximate search approach such as cube-pruning (Chiang, 2007).

Finally, we will evaluate the system using metrics such as BLEU and METEOR given that we have human-generated data. These two metrics are also used for evaluation in Konstas (2014)'s work.

However, the data we have collected is comprised of both human-generated and machine-generated texts. Therefore, we need to develop a technique to separate the two sets. One simple way is based on the Twitter username generating the tweets. In addition, we can also set up experiments comparing how different the results are when the system is trained with only human-generated texts and is trained with both sets.

Acknowledgements

The authors would like to thank the reviewers for detailed and constructive feedback. Comments and insights from Anoop Sarkar and Milan Tofiloski were also greatly appreciated in improving the quality of the paper. Special thanks to Ali Tizghadam for assistance in providing access to the necessary data. This research was supported in part by the Natural Sciences and Engineering Research Council of Canada.

References

Gabor Angeli, Percy Liang, and Dan Klein. 2010. A simple domain-independent probabilistic approach to generation. In *Proceedings of the 2010 Conference on Empirical Methods in Natural Language Processing*, EMNLP '10, pages 502–512, Stroudsburg, PA, USA. Association for Computational Linguistics.

Kalina Bontcheva and Yorick Wilks, 2004. *Automatic Report Generation from Ontologies: The MIAKT Approach*, pages 324–335. Springer Berlin Heidelberg, Berlin, Heidelberg.

David Chiang. 2007. Hierarchical phrase-based translation. *Comput. Linguist.*, 33(2):201–228, June.

T. Kasami. 1966. An efficient recognition and syntax-analysis algorithm for context-free languages. Technical Report AF-CRL-65-758, Air Force Cambridge Research Laboratory, Bedford, Massachusetts.

Joohyun Kim and Raymond J. Mooney. 2010. Generative alignment and semantic parsing for learning from ambiguous supervision. In *Proceedings of the 23rd International Conference on Computational Linguistics: Posters*, COLING '10, pages 543–551, Stroudsburg, PA, USA. Association for Computational Linguistics.

Ioannis Konstas. 2014. *Joint Models for Concept-to-Text Generation*. Ph.D. thesis, University of Edinburgh.

Eric Krokos and Hanan Samet. 2014. A look into twitter hashtag discovery and generation. In *Proceedings of the 7th ACM SIGSPATIAL Workshop on Location-Based Social Networks (LBSN14)*, Dallas, TX, Nov.

John Krumm, Robert Gruen, and Daniel Delling. 2013. From destination prediction to route prediction. *J. Locat. Based Serv.*, 7(2):98–120, June.

Percy Liang, Michael I. Jordan, and Dan Klein. 2009. Learning semantic correspondences with less supervision. In *Proceedings of the Joint Conference of the 47th Annual Meeting of the ACL and the 4th International Joint Conference on Natural Language Processing of the AFNLP: Volume 1 - Volume 1*, ACL '09, pages 91–99, Stroudsburg, PA, USA. Association for Computational Linguistics.

Lin Liao, Donald J. Patterson, Dieter Fox, and Henry Kautz. 2007. Learning and inferring transportation routines. *Artificial Intelligence*, 171(5):311 – 331.

David Lindberg, Fred Popowich, John Nesbit, and Phil Winne. 2013. Generating natural language questions to support learning on-line. *ENLG 2013*, pages 105–114.

Elena Lloret and Manuel Palomar. 2013. Towards automatic tweet generation: A comparative study from the text summarization perspective in the journalism genre. *Expert Systems with Applications*, 40(16):6624 – 6630.

Christoph Lofi and Ralf Krestel, 2012. *iParticipate: Automatic Tweet Generation from Local Government Data*, pages 295–298. Springer Berlin Heidelberg, Berlin, Heidelberg.

Natalia Marmasse and Chris Schmandt. 2000. Location-aware information delivery with commotion. In *Proceedings of the 2Nd International Symposium on Handheld and Ubiquitous Computing*, HUC '00, pages 157–171, London, UK, UK. Springer-Verlag.

Natalia Marmasse and Chris Schmandt. 2002. A user-centered location model. *Personal Ubiquitous Comput.*, 6(5-6):318–321, January.

Franois Portet, Ehud Reiter, Albert Gatt, Jim Hunter, Somayajulu Sripada, Yvonne Freer, and Cindy Sykes. 2009. Automatic generation of textual summaries from neonatal intensive care data. *Artificial Intelligence*, 173(7):789 – 816.

A. Ramos-Soto, A. J. Bugarn, S. Barro, and J. Taboada. 2015a. Linguistic descriptions for automatic generation of textual short-term weather forecasts on real prediction data. *IEEE Transactions on Fuzzy Systems*, 23(1):44–57, Feb.

A. Ramos-Soto, M. Lama, B. Vzquez-Barreiros, A. Bugarn, and M. M. S. Barro. 2015b. Towards textual reporting in learning analytics dashboards. In *2015 IEEE 15th International Conference on Advanced Learning Technologies*, pages 260–264, July.

Stuart M. Shieber, Yves Schabes, and Fernando C.N. Pereira. 1995. Computational linguistics and logic programming principles and implementation of deductive parsing. *The Journal of Logic Programming*, 24(1):3 – 36.

Priya Sidhaye and Jackie Chi Kit Cheung. 2015. Indicative tweet generation: An extractive summarization problem? In Llus Mrquez, Chris Callison-Burch, Jian Su, Daniele Pighin, and Yuval Marton, editors, *EMNLP*, pages 138–147. The Association for Computational Linguistics.

R. Simmons, B. Browning, Yilu Zhang, and V. Sadekar. 2006. Learning to predict driver route and destination intent. In *2006 IEEE Intelligent Transportation Systems Conference*, pages 127–132, Sept.

Ali Tizghadam and Alberto Leon-Garcia. 2015. Application platform for smart transportation. In *Future Access Enablers of Ubiquitous and Intelligent Infrastructures*, pages 26–32. Springer.

Yin-Yen Tseng, Jasper Knockaert, and Erik T. Verhoef. 2013. A revealed-preference study of behavioural impacts of real-time traffic information. *Transportation Research Part C: Emerging Technologies*, 30:196 – 209.

Daniel H. Younger. 1967. Recognition and parsing of context-free languages in time n^3. *Information and Control*, 10(2):189 – 208.

Analysing the Integration of Semantic Web Features for Document Planning across Genres

Marta Vicente
Department of Software
and Computing Systems
University of Alicante
Apdo. de Correos 99
E-03080, Alicante, Spain
mvicente@dlsi.ua.es

Elena Lloret
Department of Software
and Computing Systems
University of Alicante
Apdo. de Correos 99
E-03080, Alicante, Spain
elloret@dlsi.ua.es

Abstract

Language is usually studied and analysed from different disciplines generally on the premise that it constitutes a form of communication which pursues a specific objective. The discourse, in that sense, can be understood as a text which is constructed to express such objective. When a discourse is created, its production is related to some textual genre, usually connected with some pragmatic features, like the intention of the writer or the audience to whom is addressed, both conditioning the use of language. But genres can be considered as well as compounds of different pieces of text with a certain degree of order, each one seeking for more concrete objectives. This paper presents a proposal to learn such features as a way to generate richer document plans, applying clustering techniques over annotated documents.

1 Motivation and Research Context

The current research is carried out from a conception of Natural Language Generation (*NLG*) for which the creation of a text requires an intermediate output called a document plan. It is by the macroplanning stage that the system provides this plan of selected and ordered content. At present, our work is focused on how to elaborate that plan in order to meet some requisites regarding flexibility of the system: it should be able to produce different outcomes conditioned by the communicative goal, the audience,... the context, on the whole. Henceforth, the main aim of our current research is to enrich the pragmatic facet of the *NLG* process. The expected outcome is a scheme or ordering of the ideas that should be realised in a set of cohesive and coherent sentences and paragraphs.

According to some theories of the discourse (Bakhtin, 2010; Halliday et al., 2014), genres can be understood as social constructions that settle a connection between the discourse and the situation in which it is produced, reflected both in its structure and its content. According to Swavels (1990):

> "A genre comprises a class of communicative events, the members of which share some set of communicative purposes. These purposes are recognised by the expert members of the parent discourse community, and thereby constitute the rationale for the genre. This rationale shapes the schematic structure of the discourse and influences and constraints choice of content and style."

Besides, genres become interesting because they are related to communicative purposes in different manners, from a global viewpoint to fine-grained levels. As an example, we can think on the case of a person who is looking for recommendation in review pages. Recommending would be the main, global purpose of the text he consults when it was created. But it is possible that the writer also wanted to explain the motivation of the journey - narrative, personal experience - or to describe the facilities in order to complete his review. Narration, description, recommendation,... they represent low-level functions of the text related to the intention of the writer and, in some cases, they can be identified as different sets of sentences. This lead us to the possibility of learning the structure of the text and its features, which differs from one genre to another. In reviews, the presence and order of the parts is not strict.

Maybe one traveller does not share his personal story, but also he describes the room and recommends the brand, while another one first evaluates and then describes. An example to illustrate this can be found in table 1. Conversely, it would make no sense to write a scientific article that reports the results before explaining the methodology or not explaining it at all, for example.

Review 1
Personal Experience:
On our last trip to Hawaii my husband and I...
As an added bonus, we were given...
We decided to take advantage of...
Description:
The lobby is adorned with lush gardens...
Alongside the gardens are tropical birds...
The rooms are spacious.
Recommendation:
If you are ever fortunate enough to visit
the beautiful island of Kauai, try to stay
at the H Regency, you won't be disappointed.
Review 2
Description:
The W New York is on Lexington right...
The rooms are just as small as before...
The lobby of the hotel is also...
Personal Experience:
Being a corporate lawyer I travel...
The first time I was in a small room...
The second time I could not believe...
Description:
Although the room size is awful,
the hotel does have some nice touches.
Another benefit of the hotel is that...

Table 1: Review ordering from a functional approach. Just with the first words of the sentences some characteristic features can be appreciated (Verb tenses, person-thirdfirst-, ...)

Therefore, our hypothesis is that it is possible to characterise subparts of a discourse (related to a genre) according to their functionality and, at the same time, learn about its (flexible) ordering. Due to the lack of annotated corpora with discourse information about that communicative purposes, we propose to work with unsupervised techniques to achieve that goal. We expect to obtain the necessary knowledge to produce appropriate document plans. Taking into account several genres that normally exhibit a pre-defined or known-in-advance structure, such as the case of news, Wikipedia pages, or scientific article, we would be able to validate our suggested approach in other textual genres that lacks such well-defined structure a priori.

Our methodology relies on pattern detection techniques. Until now, we have tried clustering that does not require previous knowledge of the number of clusters. Over an annotated corpus we apply an Expectation-Maximisation (*EM*) algorithm, having included within the features linguistic information related to its placement.

The remainder of this paper is organised as follows. Section 2 summarises the related work concerning text classification efforts and genre studies related to communication objectives. Section 3 describes the kind of linguistic lexical features that we have been using in our experiments until now. After that, section 4 describes some resources coming from the Semantic Web environment that could complement and enrich those features. Finally, section 5 describes the experiments already performed and outlines future research opportunities.

2   Related Work

Back in 1997, Hearst tried to detect the structure of text using patterns of lexical co-occurrence to identify paragraphs related to the same topic (Hearst, 1997). In this case, term repetition proved to be enough to detect subtopics in explanatory texts, but did not include consideration about other traits of the discourse (e.g. syntactic constructions, verb tenses, number of adjectives in each region) neither recovering more meaning further than topic identification, as could be the purpose intended on the paragraph(s). Besides, the author remarked that the results had proved highly valuable when applied to explanatory text, but they would be less significant for other text types.

From another point of view, Bachand (Bachand et al., 2014) develops a research focused on the relations between text-type, discourse structures and rhetorical relations. Again, the experiments conducted are implemented on a single type of feature, this time rhetorical relations and markers. The good results obtained by the author indicate that our approach, which is grounded in similar intuitions, can reach comparable developments that we expect will enrich our capacity for generating accurate document plans.

Regarding reviews, most of the work developed refers to sentiment analysis or polarity classification (Cambria et al., 2013). A few research works have been focused on the structure related to textual genres, relying on the Systemic Functional Theory (Taboada, 2011). The relations of different parts of the text with several purposes are revealed, focusing their analysis on the domain of movie reviews, and showing at the same time the variability of the ordering in such type of documents.

Finally, a special mention must be done to the Systemic Functional Theory (Halliday et al., 2014). It provides a notion of genre that connects situation types with semantic/lexico-grammatic patterns from a conception of language highly related to its socio-semiotic origin. A textual typology is depicted on this terms, connected as well with the context of the discourse and the semantic choices to organise it (Matthiessen, 2014). On the other hand, and as a more precise example, the typology of processes that Halliday and Mathiessen describe, directly influences the classification accomplished by *ADESSE*, one of the resources applied in our experiments over Spanish reviews, explained in the next section.

3 Analysis of the Features

Having pointed out the expanse of the related work, our approach wants to overcome its limitations. On the one hand, in the sense of being suitable for any genre, not a particular one. On the other hand, focusing on several types of features at the same time, in order to propose a more comprehensive description of the parts of a discourse.

With regard to accomplish such a project, the selection and design of the proper features becomes a challenging task itself, strongly related to the aim of the investigation. Specifically, we try to detect the features that may reveal links with the functionality or purpose of the paragraph that includes them. We have begun annotating several aspects by means of linguistic tools and resources: *Freeling* (Padró and Stanilovsky, 2012) for PoS annotation and Entity Recognition and *ADESSE* (García-Miguel et al., 2010) as a source of verb senses from a semantic perspective.

4 Semantic Web to enrich the Data Set

We believe that, in order to become more meaningful, the quality of features could be improved by means of some resources rooted in Web Semantic technologies. There is some research related to genres that can be useful in our project. In the

ADESSE verb senses
Mental, material, relational, verbal, existential and modulation
FREELING features
PoS tagging: noun, adjective, pronoun, verb (tense, aspect, ...), etc.

Table 2: Features annotated over the corpus of reviews.

realm of reviews, opinion and sentiment annotation, we can take advantage for example of *MARL Ontology Specification*[1], a data schema that has been used in the *EuroSentiment Project* (Buitelaar et al., 2013) or directly related to reviews from a Sentiment Analysis perspective (Santosh and Vardhan, 2015). Other genres have been targeted for similar developments. With regard to news genre, in order to obtain more significant annotation of the documents, *BBC* provides a set of ontologies related to their contents. *DBPedia* has been already proved useful for Wikipedia articles researchers. *Drammar* (Lombardo and Damiano, 2012) and *OntoMedia* (Jewell et al., 2005) are ontology-based models for annotating features of media and cultural narratives. All of them represent resources that may lead to different results in our clustering task and analysis.

5 On-going Work

Until now, some experiments have been performed over a corpus of Spanish reviews extracted from Tripadvisor. The reviews were segmented into sentences, and some figures regarding semantic and morphological features were computed after dividing each document in regions (sets of sentences), increasing their number from one block up to four blocks of sentences. Table 3 shows some statistics of the corpus employed.

Number of reviews	1400
Sentences	12,467
Words labelled	around 200,000

Table 3: Corpus statistics.

In order to strengthen the results, corpora of other genres with different degree of flexibility in their structure are being analysed: tales, news and Wikipedia articles are to be compared with the for-

---

[1]http://www.gsi.dit.upm.es/ontologies/marl

mer outcomes. The length of the blocks is the result of a proportional division of the length of the document for now. As the research advances, new experiments will be developed to determine a more accurate size for the pseudo-paragraphs. With the ideas introduced in the section 4, our next step and proposal, includes improving the significance of the features with which the clustering algorithms have to work, trying to reveal an inner structure of the text related to its genre and purposes. The better our features are, the more precise the descriptions we can do of the discourse areas.

Acknowledgments

This research work has been supported by the Generalitat Valenciana by the grant ACIF/2016/501.It has also funded by the University of Alicante, Spanish Government and the European Commission through the projects, "Explotación y tratamiento de la información disponible en Internet para la anotación y generación de textos adaptados al usuario" (GRE13-15) and "DIIM2.0: Desarrollo de técnicas Inteligentes e Interactivas de Minería y generación de información sobre la web 2.0" (PROMETEOII/2014/001), TIN2015-65100-R, TIN2015-65136-C2-2-R, and SAM (FP7-611312), respectively.

References

Félix-Hervé Bachand, Elnaz Davoodi, and Leila Kosseim. 2014. An investigation on the influence of genres and textual organisation on the use of discourse relations. In *International Conference on Intelligent Text Processing and Computational Linguistics*, pages 454–468. Springer.

Mikhail Mikhaĭlovich Bakhtin. 2010. *Speech genres and other late essays*. University of Texas Press.

Paul Buitelaar, Mihael Arcan, Carlos Angel Iglesias Fernandez, Juan Fernando Sánchez Rada, and Carlo Strapparava. 2013. Linguistic linked data for sentiment analysis.

Erik Cambria, Bjorn Schuller, Yunqing Xia, and Catherine Havasi. 2013. New avenues in opinion mining and sentiment analysis. *IEEE Intelligent Systems*, 28(2):15–21.

José M. García-Miguel, Gael Vaamonde, and Fita González Domínguez. 2010. Adesse, a database with syntactic and semantic annotation of a corpus of spanish. In *LREC*.

MAK Halliday, Christian MIM Matthiessen, Michael Halliday, and Christian Matthiessen. 2014. *An introduction to functional grammar*. Routledge.

Marti A. Hearst. 1997. Texttiling: Segmenting text into multi-paragraph subtopic passages. *Computational linguistics*, 23(1):33–64.

Michael O. Jewell, K. Faith Lawrence, Mischa M. Tuffield, Adam Prugel-Bennett, David E. Millard, Mark S. Nixon, Nigel R. Shadbolt, et al. 2005. Ontomedia: An ontology for the representation of heterogeneous media. In *In Proceeding of SIGIR workshop on Mutlimedia Information Retrieval*. ACM SIGIR.

Vincenzo Lombardo and Rossana Damiano. 2012. Semantic annotation of narrative media objects. *Multimedia Tools and Applications*, 59(2):407–439.

Christian MIM Matthiessen. 2014. Registerial cartography: context-based mapping of text types and their rhetorical-relational organization.

Lluís Padró and Evgeny Stanilovsky. 2012. FreeLing 3.0: Towards Wider Multilinguality. In *Proceedings of the Eight International Conference on Language Resources and Evaluation (LREC'12)*. European Language Resources Association (ELRA).

D. Teja Santosh and B. Vishnu Vardhan. 2015. Feature and sentiment based linked instance rdf data towards ontology based review categorization. In *Proceedings of the World Congress on Engineering*, volume 1.

John Swales. 1990. *Genre analysis: English in academic and research settings*. Cambridge University Press.

Maite Taboada. 2011. Stages in an online review genre. *Text & Talk-An Interdisciplinary Journal of Language, Discourse & Communication Studies*, 31(2):247–269.